All
Things
New

also includes

Much Fruit
The Story of a Grain of Wheat

All Things New

also includes

Much Fruit
The Story of a Grain of Wheat

by

JESSIE PENN-LEWIS

CHRISTIAN • LITERATURE • CRUSADE
Fort Washington, Pennsylvania 19034

CHRISTIAN LITERATURE CRUSADE

U.S.A.
P.O. Box 1449, Fort Washington, PA 19034

GREAT BRITAIN
51 The Dean, Alresford, Hants., SO24 9BJ

AUSTRALIA
P.O. Box 91, Pennant Hills, N.S.W. 2120

NEW ZEALAND
10 MacArthur Street, Feilding

Originally published in England by
THE OVERCOMER LITERATURE TRUST, LTD.

First American Edition 1996
This printing 1997

ISBN 0-87508-733-7

PRINTED IN THE UNITED STATES OF AMERICA

ALL THINGS NEW

CONTENTS

MUCH FRUIT

CONTENTS

The Scripture quotes are ordinarily from the 1881 Revised Version. When from the Authorized Version (the "King James"), this is indicated. The name "Conybeare" has reference to *The Epistles of Paul* (a translation and notes) by W. J. Conybeare, England (died 1857).

The abbreviation "mg." indicates a marginal, alternative translation.

ALL THINGS NEW

Chapter 1

THE CROSS
"BEFORE THE WORLD WAS"

"The Lamb that hath been slain from the foundation of the world." (Rev. 13:8)

"Now, O Father, glorify Thou Me with the glory which I had with Thee before the world was." (John 17:5)

"God . . . who brought again from the dead the great Shepherd of the sheep, in the blood of the eternal covenant. . . ." (Heb. 13:20, margin)

IT was just after the Last Supper, where the Lord Jesus had taken bread, and broke it, and said, "This is My body which is for you: . . . In like manner also the cup, after supper, saying, This cup is the new covenant in My blood: this do, as oft as ye drink it, in remembrance of Me" (1 Cor. 11:23–26). He and His eleven disciples were on their way (see John 14:31) from the supper room to the Garden of Gethsemane. The Master continued to speak to them in the silence of the night as they passed along through the outer court of the

Temple, which was always open at midnight on the eve of the Passover. Wondrous words He spoke, so tender and full of love and understanding of the disciples' mingled feelings of sorrow and perplexity, as He speaks of a "going away," the manner of which as yet did not fully dawn upon them.

But now He stands still, and in the hush of that midnight hour lifts His eyes to heaven and pours out His heart to His Father in a prayer which gives us a glimpse into the far-back ages of eternity and the ineffable communion of the Godhead. Listen: "Having completed the work which Thou hast given Me to do . . . glorify Thou Me with the glory which I *had with Thee before the world was. . . .*"

It was no "man" who was speaking such words, but God the Son veiled in human form. The Man who stood that night and prayed was God "before the world was." He was not only Divinity but Deity. Before there was sun, or moon, or star created He was *with God.* "In the beginning was the Word, and the Word was with God, and the Word was God" (John 1:1). He was "originally in the form of God," but "counted it not a thing to be grasped to be on an equality with God but emptied Himself . . . being made in the likeness of men . . . becoming *obedient unto death,* yea, the death of the cross" (Phil. 2:6–8, mg.). He was now on the eve of that cross. The eternal covenant made between Father and Son "before the world was," which necessitated His obedience unto death, was now about to be sealed with this blood. The "Lamb slain before the foundation of the world" was now about to be slain in that world of which He was the Creator.

The purpose of the eternal covenant, made far back in that distant period of time described as "the beginning," was now about to be fulfilled. The Eternal Son has offered Himself to accomplish a work with issues so vast that as yet our finite minds can grasp but little of its vastness. The covenant concerning this work had been written in eternal records, for the Son had said, "Lo, I am come. In the roll of the book it is written of Me: I delight to do Thy will, O My God" (Psalm 40:6–8; Heb. 10:7).

What was that will? What was the subject of the covenant? A glimpse is given in the Epistle to the Colossians, in the words "For it was the good pleasure of the Father that in Him should all the fulness dwell; and *through Him to reconcile all things unto Himself,* having made peace *through the blood of His cross;* through Him, I say, whether things upon the earth, or *things in the heavens.*"* And again in Hebrews

---

*Col. 1:19–20. Conybeare remarks that the apostle suggests that "the heavenly hosts themselves stood in need of [Christ's] atonement."

9:23. "It was necessary," necessary—let us note the tone of the obligation—"that the copies of the things in the heavens should be cleansed with these [that is, the Jewish sacrifices], but *the heavenly things themselves with better sacrifices. . . .*"

It is therefore clear that the covenant made far back in eternity involved the cross, and that "before the world was" there existed some condition "in the heavens" which made a cleansing necessary, and some "reconciliation" *which only the blood of the cross could effect.* Therefore the Son of God became "the Lamb slain *before* the foundation of the world." The cross was decreed in the eternal counsels before ever the world was made and man created. It concerned realms beyond our earth planet, "things in the heavens," as well as man and "things on the earth."

All that the covenant involved, and all that the "work" meant in cost and sacrifice, the Son undertook to fulfill. A writer, deeply taught in the Scriptures, says that collective hints on this subject suggest that the Father invested the Son with special powers for the carrying out of His work, *and that the earth itself was created for this purpose.* Hence the apostle describes Him as "Primeval Creator of all creation; because in Him were all things created, in the heavens, and upon the earth, the visible and the invisible . . . all things have been created through Him and for Him . . ." (Col. 1:15–16, Worrell). And again, "All things came into being through Him" (John 1:3).

The first chapter of Hebrews seen in the light of this passage in Colossians is full of meaning, for we seem to read again of the covenant period and covenant conditions. There was a time far back in the timeless past when the Father appointed His Son, "through whom He made the ages" (Heb. 1:2, mg.), "Heir of all things" when He was "anointed . . . with the oil of gladness" above His fellows, because "He loved righteousness and *hated iniquity*"; and when the Father said to Him, "Thy Throne, O God, is for ever and ever." Then, at the moment in time when the Son, who was "very God of very God," became incarnate, the command went forth in heaven "Let all the angels of God worship Him," and all the hierarchic host of heaven worshiped at His birth. In such a birth in human form He had stripped Himself of His glory, but not of His divine nature. A "child" was born, who was at the same time "Mighty God and Everlasting Father" (Isaiah 9:6).

If we follow His steps, and listen to His words as He walked the earth as man, we find language used by Him which can only be understood in the light of the eternal covenant, indicating that He was carrying out some purpose agreed upon with His Father. "I *must* be about My Father's business," He said at the age of twelve, and later, "I *must* work the works of Him that sent Me." Nor in His hour of trial, when on the eve of the cross, could He use the authority. He had to ask for the service of angels to deliver Him, for how else could the covenant be fulfilled. So He said, "Thus it *must* be."

Again the language of One who had come from God, and who was co-equal with the Father, is used again and again: "I have *come down out of heaven.*" "The Bread of God is He who *cometh down out of heaven.*" "What if ye should behold the Son of Man ascending *where He was before?*"* And "Before Abraham existed, 'I AM,'" using the very language Jehovah used in the revelation of Himself to Moses.

The Father's delight in and witness to the Son is also full of testimony to the joy He had given to His Father's heart in the commission He had undertaken. "This is My Son, the beloved *in whom I delighted*" (Matt. 3:17, Worrell), spoke the voice from heaven at His baptism in Jordan, and repeated again on the Mount of Transfigura-

---

*See John 6:33, 38, 46, 50, 51, 58, 62, etc.

tion (Matt. 17:5). The Son also found His strength in the Father's love. "The Father loveth the Son," He said, and again in His Last Supper prayer, "Thou *lovedst Me before the foundation of the world. . . .*"

We see, therefore, that the cross was no afterthought in the counsels of Deity, but the very center or crux of an eternal covenant between the Father and the Son, made "before the world was," and that it was necessitated by some conditions in the invisible world—of which we have but glimpses—as well as being clearly necessitated by the Fall of the new human race placed on the created earth—but *foreseen and provided for* in that same covenant of the Godhead.

This is to be seen in the statements made by the Apostle Paul that the whole plan of salvation for fallen man was embodied in the eternal covenant. It was the outcome of the eternal nature of the Deity as *love*. God the Father "so loved the world that He *gave* His only begotten Son. . . ." And the Son so loved that He gave Himself. The grace of God was given "*in* Christ, before times eternal" (2 Tim. 1:9). Christ crucified as the "wisdom of God" was "foreordained before the worlds to our glory" (1 Cor. 2:7). We were chosen in Christ "before the foundation of the world" (Eph. 1:4).

Peter also says that Christ as the Lamb of God was "foreknown before the foundation of the world" (1 Pet. 1:20).

"All things" had to be "reconciled" unto the Father, and "peace" made by the blood of the cross on earth and *in heaven.* What could there be to "reconcile" or make "peace" about *in the heavens?* And what had taken place that only Deity could deal with and not one of the great archangels of God? Again we have only glimpses given in various parts of Scripture, but there are sufficient to enable us to understand. One of the highest archangels of God had fallen and drawn with him a third of the "stars" of heaven (see Rev. 12:3-4; Jude 6). An archangel of light, with the assistance of others, could cast Lucifer and his fallen angels out of the heavens (see Rev. 12:7-9), but he could never remove the effects of his fall, either in the heavens or on the earth. How painful the shock of this revolt in heaven must have been we can but dimly fathom. There was something to "reconcile" and some "peace" to restore which we cannot define or know.

Moreover, the fallen archangel himself had to be dealt with. Heaven and earth must be rid of his presence and that of the misguided ones who had chosen to follow him. He must not only be cast down from heaven but also, after his defeat at Calvary, cast out from the earth—and fallen man, who had been deceived by him, given a way back to God.

The Son—the Only Begotten of the Father—undertook the work which no archangel of God could do. The cross of Calvary set up on earth, upon which the Lamb "slain from the foundation of the world" must die, was decreed. Potentially from that moment the "Lamb" was already "slain" and forming the basis, so to speak, of all the dealings of the Holy God with the after-created universe. The principle of vicarious sacrifice was woven into the very foundations of the after-created planet earth, and life out of death was made to interpenetrate all its laws, both in nature and the world of men—not only for teaching, line upon line, the principle of vicarious sacrifice, but also to foreshow the meaning of the cross of Golgotha, when the Lamb slain from the foundation of the world would be slain before the eyes of men.

That the basis of the cross already existed in the counsels of the Deity is also to be seen in Eden (Gen. 3:21), when the first blood was shed to provide a covering for the fallen pair before sending them forth to live and toil on the sin-cursed earth.

*   *   *

When the fullness of time came, God sent forth His Son (Gal. 4:4) who, at Calvary, "delivered up" by "the determinate counsel and foreknowledge of God" (Acts 2:23), entered alone upon the conflict with the malignant foe—a conflict the issues of which concerned heaven and earth and hell. An "hour" was permitted to the "power of darkness" (Luke 22:53) in which to do its worst upon the sacrificial Lamb, and an "hour" also in which fallen man was allowed to manifest the depth of the Fall.

"Bearing the sins of the world" upon Him, the Son of God hung upon the accursed tree. The crucifixion-crime of fallen men, urged on by the invisible hosts of Satan, was on the part of the Deity a manifestation of the Lambhood nature of God; a propitiation for the sins of the whole world; and an utter overthrow of the usurper Satan and all the forces of evil. On the part of the men who crucified Him, it was no less a crime for which they were responsible because that tragic death was foreknown of God, and that it was decreed in the counsels of eternity that "God manifest in the flesh" would permit them to slay Him. These men were murderers at heart, just as Cain was "of the Wicked One," and slew his brother, for the sole reason that his works were evil and his brother's righteous. In the sight of God they also slew the Christ, even though He did not die from crucifixion but by His own voluntary laying down His life when He dismissed His spirit (Matt. 27:50).

At last from the darkness surrounding the Figure on the cross came a mighty shout of triumph. "It is finished!" He cried—and the work was done. He had put away sin by the sacrifice of Himself; He had conquered the foe. "He disarmed the principalities and the powers (which fought against Him) and put them to open shame" (Col. 2:15, Conybeare), leading them captive in His triumph. He had been "*obedient* unto death, even unto the death of the cross—wherefore also God highly exalted Him, and gave unto Him the name which is above every name; that in the name of Jesus every knee should bow, *of things in heaven,* and things on earth, and things under the earth, and that every tongue should confess that Jesus Christ is Lord to the glory of God the Father."

Chapter 2

PAUL'S FIRST SIGHT
OF THE CROSS

*"They stoned Stephen, calling upon the
Lord and saying, Lord Jesus, receive my
spirit. And he kneeled down, and cried with
a loud voice, Lord, lay not this sin to their
charge. . . ."* (Acts 7:59–60)

*"And the witnesses laid down their
clothes at a young man's feet, whose name
was Saul."* (Acts 7:58)

*"And Saul was consenting unto his
death."* (Acts 8:1)

THE saying "The blood of the martyrs is
the seed of the Church" was never more
exemplified than in the death of the first
Christian martyr. And little did that martyr know that in his death, and in the manner of it, to another standing by would be
given a glimpse of the Calvary of his Lord.
For the Calvary of the God-Man did not
consist only of the wooden cross and the
nails and the laid-down life. Its inner es-
sence and power was the spirit of it, manifested peculiarly in the words which came
from the Sufferer in the midst of His agony,
"Father forgive them. . . ."

It was this spirit of the Lamb slain which Saul caught sight of in Stephen. In the midst of the agony of a death by stoning, bruised and bleeding, there breaks out from him the prayer for his murderers, "Lord, lay not this sin to their charge." It was Calvary re-enacted before the eyes of one who afterwards would himself receive that same spirit and become a God-empowered messenger of the cross. Saul could never forget the sight of the true character of Jesus which he must have caught that day. Nor would the Holy Spirit who was then in the midst of the apostles in mighty power cease to keep it before him, until on the way to Damascus he met the Risen Lord and knew in truth that He who had been slain was indeed the Living One, and had chosen him also to be His witness and to suffer many things for His name's sake.

That Saul should be specially named in connection with the death of Stephen is not without a purpose in the mind of the Holy Spirit. This young man was even then a "chosen vessel." He had already been fully trained in the Jewish Scriptures, at the feet of Gamaliel. His "theological course," so to speak, was practically finished. It was not intellectual "knowledge" that he now needed to make him a fit messenger of Christ, but a direct revelation of Christ, both as the Lamb slain and as the Living One who "became dead" and "alive for evermore."

Calvary itself could not be re-enacted, since He who had died had died once for all, and ascended to heaven. But it was necessary that this man, chosen so specially to be the Apostle of the Cross, should not only know of the Calvary message from the Scriptures, and from the lips of the Lord Himself, but *he needs must see it in its inner spirit* when manifested in a human life. Stephen was chosen by God for this purpose. The forgiving spirit of Jesus manifested on the cross was manifested in him so that the chosen messenger of that cross might have the same spirit infused into his own heart and life. For the preaching of the cross needs the *spirit* of the cross behind the message if it is not to be made void by the preacher.

That this sudden insight into the heart of the cross *is* possible we know in experience, for have we not sometimes seen, for just a brief moment, a shining out of the spirit of the Lamb of Calvary in another child of God—a shining which in some inexplicable way *suddenly opened the very depths of Calvary to us* and gave us penetrating insight into its inner spirit . . . which never again is lost, but has a formative influence upon us for the rest of our mortal life?

Moreover, that strange, sudden glimpse of the Lamb-spirit searched the very depths of our innermost life in deep convicting power, which could not be gainsaid or withstood in its divine revelation. Just as, for example, that one look from the silent Lord as He stood before His persecutors in the high priest's palace worked deeply in Peter, bringing him to himself and breaking his heart.

It seems to have been thus with the young man Saul. The record of his raging persecution of the saints after Stephen's death in no wise alters the fact that he had seen the outshining of the glory of God in the disposition of Christ in Stephen, and had, unrealized at the time, met with the Lamb of Calvary in His martyred servant even before he was arrested by the Lord from heaven on the Damascus road. "It is hard for thee to kick against the pricks," said the One who had been watching the working of His Spirit in him, and Saul, who found his heart laid bare, had nothing to explain.

We see, therefore, that the glimpse of Calvary given to Saul in Stephen's death was preparation for meeting with the Risen Lord on the way to Damascus, as well as giving to the "chosen vessel" that insight into the inner meaning of the cross which afterwards so characterized his life and enabled him long years later to read in his own persecutions and afflictions the outworking of the same inner principle of the cross.

That day it was a glimpse of Calvary *by reflection*, but years afterward he had drunk so deeply of the same spirit that he could say he "gloried" in the cross of Christ, and that its offense was now his "proudest boast" (Gal. 6:14, Lightfoot).

Then, as the years went by, the yearning to have the deepest meaning of the cross wrought out in his own life became so intensified that, when he wrote to the Philippians, his cry was that the whole of his being should be brought under the power of that death. "That I may know Him," he said, "and the power of His resurrection, and the fellowship of His sufferings, being made conformable to His death . . ." (Phil. 3:10).

From first to last the spirit of Calvary that Paul caught a sight of in Stephen, and afterwards learned to understand by the teaching of the Lord Himself, was reproduced in his own life. Its very preaching became the instrument of his own crucifixion. "The cross of Christ is the instrument of my crucifixion as of His, for I am crucified with Him,"* said the apostle, so that by that inwrought working of the death of Christ, caused by the suffering brought about through the cross he proclaimed, he was "crucified to the world" in his innermost life as the Lord had been at Golgotha when, rejected and despised by the world of men, He passed to another world through the gateway of death.

"God forbid that I should glory in anything save in the cross of Christ. On that cross I have been crucified to the world, and the world has been crucified to me. Henceforth we are dead to each other," cries the apostle. "For I think God hath set forth us the apostles last of all, as men doomed to death; for we are made a spectacle unto the world, both to angels and to men. . . . We are made as the filth of the world, the offscouring of all things, even until now" (see 1 Cor. 4:9–13).

---

*Lightfoot on Galatians.

Chapter 3

THE CROSS
REVEALED BY CHRIST

*"I certify you, brethren, that the gospel
which was preached of me is not after man.
For I neither received it of man, neither was
I taught it, but by the revelation of Jesus
Christ."* (Gal. 1:11–12, A.V.)
*"That the God of our Lord Jesus Christ . . .
may give . . . the spirit of wisdom and rev-
elation. . . ."* (Eph. 1:17)

THE cross of Calvary can only be truly
understood in the light of the utter ruin
of man in the Fall, and the extent of the
Fall of man can only be seen in the light of
Calvary. Moreover, the knowledge of sin as
it is in the sight of God can come to men
who are blinded by the Fall and darkened
in their understanding only by the convicting of the Holy Spirit of God. And the
knowledge of the remedy in the propitiatory sacrifice of the Son of God on the cross
of Calvary can come only by the same convicting power of the Holy Spirit.

It was thus "by revelation" that the gospel of the cross came to this once self-righ-

teous Pharisee and made him, at the very end of a magnificent life, call himself "the chief of sinners" even though "as touching the righteousness which is in the law" he was "blameless."

"It came to me *through revelation of Jesus Christ*," writes the apostle as to the gospel which he preached. "*I did not receive it from man*," nor is it "*after man*," he emphasizes. He goes on to say how he conferred not with flesh and blood after his meeting with the Risen Lord on the road to Damascus, but after a bold testimony to Christ in the very city where he had meant to persecute His followers he went to Arabia, where, for a period not clearly recorded, he appears to have remained in retirement. It was doubtless at this time that the Ascended Lord unfolded to him the gospel by direct revelation, and it was only after this that he went up to Jerusalem to become acquainted with Peter.

It was not until fourteen years later that he was bidden, again "by revelation," to go up to Jerusalem to lay before the other apostles the gospel which had been given him to preach among the Gentiles.

How truly Paul had been given his message of the cross by the Lord Jesus is seen in the fact that the apostles in Jerusalem had "nothing to impart" (Gal. 2:6) to him regarding the gospel they had learned from the Lord Jesus Himself after His resurrection when He opened the Scriptures to them. Jesus had showed them "the things concerning Himself" written in "Moses," which includes Genesis *with its history of the Fall*; in "the prophets," including Isaiah, with the fifty-third chapter giving the foreshadowed portrait of the propitiatory sacrifice of the Lamb of God; and in the Psalms, including the twenty-second, foreshowing the sufferings of Christ in His death at Calvary.

So entirely in harmony was the gospel opened to the apostles by the Risen Christ *before* His ascension with the gospel given to the Apostle Paul by the Ascended Christ, that Peter, James and John, the pillars of the church, did not hesitate to give the right hand of fellowship to the former Pharisee who had once so zealously sent the saints to death, determined to stamp out the heresy of the followers of the Nazarene.

The gospel revealed to and preached by Paul is, therefore, by these recorded facts, proved to be entirely in accordance with the gospel proclaimed by Peter, James and John, the three who had lived and walked so intimately with the Son of God in the days of His flesh; the three who had been with Him on the Mount of Transfiguration and in the Garden of Gethsemane; men who had seen Him and eaten with Him after He rose from the dead; men who knew Christ's gospel from the lips of the Lord Himself, and therefore men who could quickly detect aught that was "after man" in any "gospel" placed before them by another.

We cannot today emphasize the tremendous fact too strongly, that Paul's gospel of the cross as opened out in his epistles is therefore *the Ascended Lord's own explanation of the meaning of His cross*, given by Him to His church through His chosen vessel Paul; and is the very same gospel which He opened to the disciples just after His resurrection, when He showed them in the books of Moses and the prophets the things concerning Himself. The Risen Christ, while yet on earth, explaining His sufferings as foreshown in the Old Testament Scriptures, and the Ascended Lord Christ explaining His cross and passion and glorious resurrection to the man who was thoroughly trained as a strict Pharisee in the same Old Testament Scriptures, is *one and the same Lord, speaking the same thing.*

What the Risen Lord opened in the Old Testament Scriptures to His disciples on the road to Emmaus is not left in mystery, for the line of His unfolding and interpretation we find in His word "Behoved it not the Christ to suffer these things, and to enter into His glory?" and "Thus it is written, that the Christ should suffer, and rise again from the dead the third day" (Luke 24:26, 46).

"*It came to me by revelation,*" said Paul, and it comes so still to every member of the fallen race. It was by "revelation," described as the "opening of their understanding," that the gospel of the cross came to the two on the way to Emmaus; and to the company assembled in Jerusalem, when they were "shown" the things in the Scriptures concerning the suffering Messiah by that same Messiah who had died in fulfillment of those prophecies, and had risen from the dead.

If the disciples who had been taught by Christ for three years needed the "opening of their understanding" by the Risen Lord, how much more all other men? "By revelation," described by Paul as "the eyes of your understanding filled with light" (Eph. 1:18, Conybeare), must the same insight into the message of the cross come to every soul, for "the natural man receiveth not the things of the Spirit of God," they are foolishness unto him, and "he cannot know them because they are spiritually discerned" (1 Cor. 2:14).

Moreover, if a Paul, taught in the Old Testament Scriptures as only a Pharisee could be, and with a gigantic intellect trained in all the theological subtleties of the Jews, needed "revelation," how much more do we? And if the gospel as given by the Christ Himself to His apostles is a "revelation" of God, as we see it is, can it today be swept aside as of no account without appalling loss? A man that set at nought Moses' law died without mercy; "of how much sorer punishment, think ye, shall he be judged worthy, who hath trodden under foot the Son of God, and hath counted the blood of the covenant . . . a common thing?" (Heb. 10:28–29, mg.).

"By revelation" shall we know the true meaning of the cross in these days when the foundations of all things are being shaken.

"Now I see," writes a minister of the gospel, "that the cross is not to be understood by mere study, but by a divine unveiling. Behold, I talk as if it were *new*, yet a thing known me from childhood! Ah, no, it was not known, only *thought* to be known. It was a subject so familiar that it could be debated about, but not so real as to make debating about it folly.

"Now I see the cross is only known in the light of the Spirit. To the carnal mind of the mere intellectualist it must remain a stumbling block and foolishness. I have been trying to remove the 'stumbling block,' and to convert the 'foolishness' into wisdom acceptable to carnal-minded hearers by endless explanations, but now I see clearly that the 'Jew' and the 'Greek' must be converted. When the Jew is willing to open his eyes, and the Greek becomes a little child, the stumbling block will become the steppingstone to the throne, and the 'foolishness' the very wisdom of God. . . ."

Chapter 4

THE CROSS
IN THE LIGHT OF THE FALL

"Him who knew no sin He made . . . sin on our behalf; that we might become the righteousness of God in Him." (2 Cor. 5:21)

"Christ also suffered for sins once, the righteous for the unrighteous, . . . being put to death in the flesh, but quickened in the spirit. . . ." (1 Peter 3:18)

"The ark . . . wherein few, that is, eight souls, were saved through water. . . ." (1 Peter 3:20)

"THE gospel which was preached of me was not after man" is a truth that very specially needs to be emphasized as we turn to the theme of this chapter, for Paul's teaching about the Fall of man (Rom. 5:12–14), and the utter ruin of the first creation, was Christ's own revelation to him concerning man's condition. So also the deep inner meaning of His substitutionary death on the cross.

To see the cross in its wonderful fitness to the deepest need of man, we must, so to speak, retire from it back to the earliest records of human history; and then from that perspective we shall see very clearly the purposes of God in giving His Son to be an offering for sin, a propitiatory sacrifice for the sins of the whole world (Rom. 3:25; 1 John 2:2).

In the sixth chapter of Genesis it is written: "And the Lord saw that the wickedness of man was great, . . . that every imagination of the thoughts of his heart was only evil continually" (Gen. 6:5). And this was written of the race of man concerning whom God had said in the beginning: "Let Us make man in Our image"! This same race of man had fallen from bad to worse after the Fall in the Garden of Eden, until the Creator "repented that He had made man . . . for it grieved Him at His heart" (Gen. 6:6).

Here we see sin as a wound to the heart of the Creator. Not sin merely as a lapse from God, or sin in the abstract as a vile thing; but sin *in relation to God,* grieving the heart of a Divine Person who had created man in His own likeness, to have dominion over the earth; and who had rejoiced in His handiwork, and lovingly made provision for the happiness of the creature He had formed to walk in fellowship with Himself.

Looking upon the fair earth and the man

He had created to rule over it, He sees him no longer as the spiritual being with whom He had once communed in the Garden of Eden. "My Spirit shall not rule in man . . . for in their going astray *they are flesh*" (Gen. 6:3, mg.), He said. Then came from the holy God the only decision that could be in accordance with His character. The Lord said, "I will destroy man," or "blot out" mankind (Gen. 6:7, mg.).

Choosing one family as a new center, so to speak, for the renewal of the race, He speaks to Noah and makes known to him His purpose: "I do bring the flood of waters upon the earth to destroy all flesh" (Gen. 6:17), for "every living thing that I have made will I destroy" or "blot out" (Gen. 7:4, mg.), the Creator said.

How Noah and his family alone were saved in an ark which had been built under the direction of Jehovah Himself, and how the flood came, and everything living was "blotted out from the earth" (v. 23, mg.) the seventh chapter of Genesis records, and the extent of the destruction shows the utter ruin of man in the Fall, although originally created in the image of God.

The expression "blotted out"* is deeply

---

*In using these marginal renderings of the text, it should be remembered that no Old Testament type of New Testament truth can be pressed to analogy in every detail. Every type gives but one aspect of a truth, which would require many other types to depict its full meaning.

suggestive and significant when considered in the typical meaning of the flood. Let us not fail to note that it was "all *flesh*" that was thus dealt with; not fallen man as a personal entity, who will yet stand before God for judgment in that day when every man will give account of himself to God (see Rev. 20:12). They who were "disobedient in the days of Noah" appear to be yet "spirits in prison" awaiting that day (1 Pet. 3:19–20).

How deep and irremediable was the Fall in Eden is proved in that even the race born from the family of Noah after the flood is found to have the poison of the serpent still in them, and to be capable of such depths of corruption that, thousands of years afterwards, in spite of Roman civilization and culture, the Apostle Paul gives a picture in Roman 1:18–32 probably quite as black as the condition of the pre-flood days of Noah. That no civilization, and no "culture," no moral law, no teaching, and no training removes the poison of the serpent is plainly seen both in Paul's description of the innate sinfulness of man as given in the earlier chapters of Romans and in the twentieth century record of crime and sin which is covered over by the artificial civilization of today.

The Apostle Paul sums up the whole race

under sin, and he proves it to be guilty before God of sin against the holy and loving Creator. *"I will 'blot out' man,"* said the Creator in the days of Noah, and He blotted him out by the flood—that is, man as *fallen flesh*, but not as a *spirit* which must live forever. *"I will blot out man"* is still the only alternative of the Creator as He looks at the fallen race after the flood, but this time the verdict will be carried out in another way, a way of which the flood in the days of Noah *was actually the type*—a way which had been planned in the council of eternity "before the world was," by a God of infinite holiness and infinite love, hating the sin and loving the sinner. He will "blot out" corrupt and fallen "flesh" by a flood of judgment on His own Son, who, in the fullness of time, would come in the "likeness of flesh of sin" (see Rom. 8:3, mg.), and being "made sin" on the sinner's behalf, would take the sins of the whole world upon Him, and carry to the cross in His own person as the Substitute the sinful and fallen Adam race: where lifted up upon a cross between earth and heaven, as a spectacle to angels and to men, the fallen flesh is put to death in the person of the Representative Man, being proved before angels and man as having sinned beyond repair.

A glimpse into this meaning of the cross

is given by Peter, who shows that the flood itself was a type of baptism—the flood of water typifying the judgment-death of Christ, and "eight souls saved through water" (see 1 Pet. 3:18–21) by being borne in the ark on the waters of death into a new world and a new life. Baptism is therefore clearly a type, and one of the many figures used to depict the Calvary death, and the submerging there of the old Adam-life of each one who enters the Ark—Christ—to pass in Him to a new world and a new life.

The knowledge, then, of the ruin of the Fall is fundamentally necessary for the apprehension of the marvelous fitness and perfect remedy set forth in the cross of Calvary. Potentially, man as the old creation in Adam is put to death in Christ on the cross, so that in Christ as the Second Adam he may be re-created (1) by a new birth unto righteousness (1 Pet. 2:24); (2) by receiving a new life in union with the Lord from heaven; and (3) being translated into a new sphere of the kingdom of the Son (Col. 1:13).

The new life for the children of the fallen race is potentially true for every soul born into the world, only to become actually true by individual faith and appropriation. "To as many as received Him [and only such] is given the right to become children of God" (John 1:12).

The awful fact of the Fall, and the cross of Christ as the complementary answer to it, needs to be *revealed* to each member of the fallen race by the power of the Holy Spirit. Even the man who is blameless and upright like Job needs to be brought to the cry "Behold, I am vile. I abhor myself" (Job 40:4; 42:6). The zealous religious man who is "touching the righteousness which is in the law, blameless"—like Saul the Pharisee—needs to be brought to say, "I know that in me, that is, in my flesh, dwelleth no good thing" (Rom. 7:18), for "There is none righteous, *no, not one. . . .*"

"Revelation," and only "revelation" by God Himself, can accomplish the undeceiving of the fallen race, as "revelation" brought it to pass in Job and Paul. For it is written: "The god of this age hath blinded the minds [*thoughts*, mg.] of the unbelieving, that the light of the gospel of the glory of Christ, who is the image of God, should not dawn upon them" (2 Cor. 4:4).

The extent of the apprehension of the depth and utter ruin of the first-Adam nature caused by the Fall *determines the extent of the experiential knowledge of the new birth*, and the imparted life of Christ. It determines also the extent to which the new life in Christ can be brought to full growth in the believer, for just so far as the man clings to one supposed "good thing" in him, so far the power of the cross is nullified in his life, and so far the growth of the new life is hindered in him. Moreover, it especially determines the extent of the apprehension of that aspect of the cross set forth in the sixth of Romans, where the apostle declares of the cross, "Our old man was crucified with Him that the body of sin might be done away. . . ," for nothing but the recognition of the "old man," the fallen humanity, as *corrupt in toto*, will lead the believer to "cast off" the "*whole body of the flesh*" as crucified with Christ, that he might become a new creation.

In brief, from every viewpoint, the recognition of the Fall of man is the basic truth for the understanding of the dealings of God with man, revealed to us in the Scriptures, and only from this deep bedrock base can the Scriptures themselves be understood. If we cast aside this revealed truth, the whole edifice of Scripture teaching falls to pieces, as having no foundation.

Apart from the key of the Fall the blood-shedding of the sacrifices in Israel had no meaning, nor has the cross erected on Golgotha any delivering message to man today, nor at any time in the history of the race.

Moreover, the necessity of recognizing the fact of the Fall lies at the very core of victory over sin and Satan. Self-deception *here* is obviously the blinding work of the devil, for let the Deceiver persuade a man that in his own nature dwelleth some "good thing," he beguiles him to retain some part of the old fallen creation wherein evil spirits can find their workshop.

Victory over sin and Satan is the message of the cross, but it can only be realized in experience up to the extent of the believer's recognition of the Fall, and a consequent offcasting of the fallen life of the first Adam at the place called Calvary.

Chapter 5

THE CROSS
AND THE CURSE OF THE TREE

"Christ redeemed us from the curse of the law, having become a curse for us. . . ." (Gal. 3:13)

"He that is hanged is the curse of God." (Deut. 21:23, mg.)

"[Jesus] they slew, hanging Him on a tree." (Acts 10:39)

THE Apostle Paul, in writing to the Galatians, quotes these words from the Old Testament Scriptures, and bases upon them a fundamental truth concerning the Lord Jesus and His death on Calvary. Again let us say as we read them, "This is *the Lord's own interpretation of His death.*" The exact words in Deuteronomy are very striking. "He that is hanged is accursed of God," or "the curse of God" (Deut. 21:23, mg.). The holy, sinless Son of God (Heb. 4:15) "hung on a tree," was then, by the law of Moses, made the "curse of God."

The Jews who crucified Him knew this, and, as a writer once pointed out, thought they had effectually ended His claim to be the Messiah by thus nailing Him to a tree. They argued that one who was "accursed of God" by such a death could not be accepted by the people as the Anointed Messiah.

The leaders of the Jews were blinded and did not realize that they were actually *fulfilling the Law* when they crucified the Man called Jesus. The key of substitution was the only one to unlock the mystery of a Man being "cursed" of God and "blessed" at one and the same time. Paul, deeply taught in "the Jews' religion," and afterwards taught by Christ the things concerning Himself in the Hebrew Scriptures, interpreted the truth of this mysterious paradox in the words "Christ redeemed us from the curse of the law, *having become a curse for us.*"

To understand the curse of the law we must read the terrible words in Deuteronomy, written in chapters 27:15–26; 28:15–68; 29:1–29, with chapter 30 giving Moses' appeal to Israel. The apostle applies these curses of the law not only to Israel, but to all men, when he says, "As many as are of the works of the law are under a curse: for it is written, Cursed is every one which continueth not in all things that are written in the book of the law, to do them" (Gal. 3:10). The curse of the broken law rests upon all men, and escape from that curse is only through faith-union with Him who became a curse for us.

Moses was commanded by God to teach the children of Israel, as part of the statutes and commandments given on the Mount for their obedience, that any man who was hung on a tree was under God's curse.

Now why should God reveal to Moses on the fiery Mount that a man hung on a tree was peculiarly under His curse, any more than a man who was slain in a field, or a man who was drowned in a pit, or who died any other violent form of death? Was not this statute given to Israel as a foreshadowing of the purpose of the cross, and was not the meaning of this aspect of the cross one of "the things concerning Himself" which the Risen Lord opened to the two disciples on the way to Emmaus?

The depth of the Fall of man is seen in that the Man representing the whole of our fallen race must die on the tree. His death in Gethsemane, or in any other way than on the cross, would not have been a full complement to the Fall, because the Fall involved the curse, and "It is written," said the apostle, "*cursed* is every one that hangeth on a tree"!

In harmony with this opening of the Scriptures, it is striking to find in the ear-

liest record of the message proclaimed by
the apostles after Pentecost that they were
constantly referring to Christ as having
been "hung on a tree." "Ye slew, and
hanged on a tree," said the apostles fear-
lessly to the high priest of Israel (Acts 5:30).
"Whom they slew, and *hanged on a tree,*
Him God hath raised up," Peter said again
to Cornelius (Acts 10:39–40), having no
hesitation in boldly stating about Christ
the most repugnant thing that could be
said about Him to a Jew.

The Lord Jehovah who gave this statute
to Moses to convey to Israel was the very
same God who said in the days of Noah, "I
will blot out man from the earth"; and the
very same God who in the fullness of time
sent His Son—who "by the determinate
counsel and foreknowledge of God" (Acts
2:23) was hung upon a tree and slain.
Behold Him there, "the curse of God," because the curse of God was upon the fallen
race of Adam! "Having become a curse *for
us,*" the Christ, the Son of the Blessed, became a curse in our stead; therefore,
Calvary's tree means blessing and cursing,
not only to Him who hung there *but to all
others of the human race.*

His death as an example of sacrifice, or
even as a manifestation of the love of God,
would not have been the remedy, nor the

answer to the Fall. Nor was it the satisfying of the vengeance of an angry God. Nay, nay. Far deeper lies the cause and meaning of the cross of Calvary. The death of Calvary was God's only way to save the world. Propitiation! Yes—for sin against a holy God needs the atonement of blood; but it also requires the carrying of the fallen Adam to that cross, cursed and corrupted beyond repair. Yea, and far, far deeper lies the meaning of the death of the cross in the counsels of God. Far, far wider than the scope of the little planet of earth lies the need for and purpose of the cross.

The world of *fallen angels,* who have been cast out of heaven for their sin and pride and disobedience—these look on to see how a holy God will deal with a fallen creature; and a host of *unfallen beings* around the throne of God wait with eager desire to know (1 Pet. 1:12) how the Lord God Almighty, whom they worship, crying "Holy, Holy, Holy," will retain His holy character and yet reveal His nature of love.

Behold the wondrous mystery! See the wisdom of God! See the fallen creature in the person of His Substitute, with the curse of the holy God upon Him, hanging in full view of earth and heaven, in view of the fallen angels and the unfallen angelic beings around the throne. See hung upon a tree, and thereby "accursed of God," the person of the sinless Son of God, who came to earth in the "likeness of sinful flesh" and carried it to the tree with the curse of God upon it; condemned to death, even the death of the cross.

But there is yet *more* in the cross of Calvary and the statement that Christ redeemed us from the curse of the law, having become a curse for us. In Genesis 3:14 we find that the curse of God was passed upon Satan when, in Eden, in the form of a serpent, he approached the innocent woman and beguiled her in his craftiness. That *curse remains upon him*; and all who become identified with him must share in the consequences of that curse* if they refuse to accept the salvation open to them through the death of the Son of God. They too become finally accursed, and are sent to share his doom.

Man has not only to escape from the curse of a broken law but from partaking of the consequences of the curse upon Satan—the first cause of all sin and rebellion against God. The one place of escape is Calvary. There alone, through the substitution of the Holy One upon the tree as "The Curse of God," is man redeemed from the curse pronounced by the law and brought back into fellowship with God.

---

*See Matt. 25:41; John 8:44; 1 John 3:8; Rev. 20:10, 14–15.

There alone, by identification with the One upon the tree, "accursed of God," is the accursed fallen nature, poisoned by the serpent, continuously "brought to nought" (Rom. 6:6, Worrell) and the new man in Christ enabled to walk in newness of life— free from the curse of the broken law and made free from participation in the curse of the serpent, by union with the risen life of Him who became a curse for us.

So solemn is the consequence of mini-mizing the message and the results of the rejection of this gospel that a curse is even pronounced upon those who substitute any other "gospel" in its place. "Though we, or an angel from heaven, preach any other gospel unto you than that which we have preached unto you"—that is, the gospel of the cross, and the Christ bearing the curse of sin—"let him be accursed," wrote the Apostle Paul to the Galatians (Gal. 1:8, A.V.). Yes, because any other "gospel" than that of Calvary's substitutionary death of the Son of God as the Curse-Bearer leaves *the curse of God upon men unrevoked.* "Let him be *what he is,*" in effect said the apostle,"*accursed,*" for either he or the Man of Calvary must bear the curse of God on sin and Satan. "*All* who are of the works of the law" are "under a curse"; that is, all who rely upon their own obedience to the law, their own moral attainments, their own "good works." "Under a curse." Ah, how little we understand God's view of sin: "There is none that doeth good, no, not one." The broken law which brings the curse shuts up all men "under sin." Let us flee to Calvary, and there escape from the cursed fallen life of Adam *into* Him who became a curse for us.

Chapter 6

THE CROSS
AND THE FALLEN WISDOM

"The word of the cross is to them that are perishing foolishness; but unto us which are being saved it is the power of God. For it is written, I will destroy the wisdom of the wise. . . ." (1 Cor. 1:18–19)

"If ye have bitter jealousy and faction . . . this wisdom is not a wisdom which cometh down from above, but is earthly, natural, demoniacal. . . ." (James 3:14–15, mg.)

THE cross is not only God's complete answer to the Fall, but it is also His chosen weapon for dealing with its effect in the human race. The original cause of sin was the serpent, as he whispered, "Ye shall be as God," but the open door for the entry of sin was found in the woman's understandable desire for knowledge. "The woman saw that the tree was to be desired to *make one wise . . .*" (Gen. 3:5–6).

It was therefore through the avenue of the intellect that sin entered the world. The Fall ended in gross flesh in the days of Noah, but it began in Eden in that part of man which distinguished him from the beasts, in his power to reason, to think, and to gain knowledge. "The tree was to be desired to make one *wise*," we read, but it would be wisdom gained outside the limit of God's permission. It was the "tree of the knowledge of good and *evil*" (Gen. 2:17); therefore *evil existed before the creation of man*. Other parts of Scripture reveal that the evil was in the supernatural realm, and had first broken out among the angels of God. If the innocent pair were to eat of that tree it would bring upon them *knowledge of the evil already existing in the spiritual sphere*, and open the door to that "evil" entering them—as in truth it did.

Satan, in the form of the serpent, gained his entrance into the new race by beguiling them into the same sin against God which brought about his own fall. "Ye shall be *as God*, knowing good and evil," said the crafty foe. Who would not be *like God* if he could? How proper it seemed to desire to be wise, but God knew there was danger in the knowledge of the evil which *then existed only among the fallen angels*.

"I will be like the Most High" was the language of Satan when he revolted against his Creator. It has been suggested that this was at the time when the Only Begotten Son was "exalted above all the heavenly powers, and received a more excellent name than they," when "by divine affiliation He became partaker of the infinite power, wisdom and authority," and when He was appointed "Heir of all things," and all the inhabitants of heaven were bidden to acknowledge His supremacy. We might well suppose this greatest of the archangels saying, "I, too, will be like the Most High," and refusing to bow to the edict of the Creator. If this was so it would explain why he was, and has been even unto this day, the bitter and malignant foe of the Only Begotten of the Father. Against Him was all his malice directed and his schemes planned from the earliest point of history, right down to the hour when the fallen archangel was "cast out" from his position as prince of this world, at Calvary.

The apostle's reference, in his second epistle to the Corinthians, to the Fall in Eden, shows that the serpent, in his craftiness, gained entrance into Eve through the *mind*, or *thoughts* (2 Cor. 11:3, mg.). Hence man's intellect is as fallen as the rest of his nature. Listen to the apostle who was once a rigid Pharisee—"as touching the righteousness which is in the law, found blameless"—as he says about himself, as well as all other men: "We all once lived . . . doing the desires of the flesh and of the

mind [*thoughts*, mg.], and were by nature
children of wrath . . ." (Eph. 2:3).

Man is, consequently, so darkened in his
understanding (Eph. 4:18) that the things
of the Spirit are foolishness to him, and he
cannot know them. He has lost that spirit-
perception and power of spirit-apprehen-
sion which Adam had before he fell, and
which enabled him to have fellowship with
God.

The divine purpose "I will blot out man"
in his fallen condition, as declared and
carried out in type by the flood, and fulfilled for the whole fallen race by the death
of Christ on the cross, *includes man's wisdom* and man's attempt to know God by
means of the "wisdom of the world," con-
ceived and evolved by the fallen intellect.

Hence the cross is not only the answer
to the Fall, in the old fallen creation being
carried to the cross of death in the person
of the Substitute; but in its message, and
acceptance individually, it is "the power of
God" to destroy "the wisdom of the wise,"
that is, the fallen wisdom of the natural
man, which is "foolishness with God."
Man's fallen "wisdom" is destroyed by the
word of the cross, when he submits to the
wisdom of the Creator and humbly accepts
salvation and redemption through that
cross.

The "word of the cross, to them that are perishing, is foolishness"—to the wisdom of man; but the "foolishness of God"—in what man calls the "folly" of salvation through the death of Another on a cross—is "wiser than man"; for through the very message of the cross, the Creator destroys the fallen wisdom which keeps men from the true wisdom of God.

Moreover, God makes "foolish" in the eyes of the world the fallen wisdom of man—by saving from the depths of sin all who accept His salvation through the cross; thus accomplishing before the eyes of men what the fallen wisdom fails to accomplish by all its reasoning and all its schemes to "save" men, built up by the intellect of man. Yes, countless times has God made "foolish" the wisdom of the world in the eyes of men by lifting up sinners sunk in the depths of sin through simple faith in the message of the cross.

"O the depths of the riches, both of the wisdom and knowledge of God! How unsearchable are His judgments, and His ways past finding out!" The cross is God's wisdom, planned far back in the ages of eternity, before "the foundation of the world," as His one weapon for dealing with (1) the fall of the archangel in heaven, Satan, and all its terrible results in the invisible world; and (2) the fall of the human race in its federal head, Adam, and all its terrible results on earth.

Not only is man's intellect fallen, and his wisdom "foolishness" with God, but it is plainly said that the satanic power which was the origin of his fall continues to *hold the darkened understanding under a veil* which prevents the light of the gospel of the cross penetrating it: "The god of this world hath blinded the minds [*thoughts*, mg.] ... that they should not see the light ..." (2 Cor. 4:4). It does not say that the devil merely blinds the mind of the atheist, the degraded, the uneducated, or the poor, but the "*unbelieving*"—just as surely including all men in their natural state, whether prince or professor, rich or poor, bond or free.

The proclamation of the cross is God's weapon, and the only weapon able to remove this satanic veil upon the fallen intellect; hence the devil's consistent and persistent omission of the message of the cross in all religions evolved from that darkened intellect—not even excepting those who bear the name "Christian" while omitting the very message of Christ who came from heaven to give Himself a ransom for all. The mind blinded by Satan is made to reject the cross; revolt against the cross; tone down the meaning of the cross; shrink from the language of the cross—all because the Deceiver of men knows that the "word of the cross" as the "power of God" will, by the working of the Spirit of God, destroy his veil and make men see that the "natural man" cannot receive the things of the Spirit of God because they are spiritually discerned. Not until this veil upon the mind is removed will there dawn upon the darkened mind of Jew or Greek the true wisdom of God in the cross— "Christ crucified, unto Jews a stumbling block, and unto Gentiles foolishness, but unto the called themselves, both Jews and Greeks, Christ the power of God and the *Wisdom of God*" (1 Cor. 1:23–24, mg.).

Chapter 7

THE CROSS
AND THE SERPENT

*"Now shall the prince of this world be cast
out. And I, if I be lifted up from the earth,
will draw all men unto Me."* (John 12:31–
32)

*"That through death He might bring to
nought him that had the power of death,
that is, the devil. . . ."* (Heb. 2:14)

*"Who delivered us out of the power of
darkness, and translated us into the kingdom of the Son of His love; in whom we
have our redemption."* (Col. 1:13–14)

HERE we have the cross in its relation
to the devil stated in unequivocal language. Calvary had tremendous consequences for him whom the Lord described
as "the prince of this world," in terms which
acknowledged him to be a person of un-
doubted authority and influence. A
"prince," and yet called a *serpent* because
of his having taken the serpent's form in
Eden; a "prince" and yet a deceiver of the
whole inhabited earth (Rev. 12:9).

The cross means not only the putting to
death of the fallen creation poisoned by the

59

serpent and the birth there of a new race, but it eventually brings about the "bringing to nought"—to use the exact language of Scripture—of the serpent who was the original cause of the Fall. This is wonderfully depicted in the foreshadowing of the cross given in the lifting up of the serpent in the wilderness, and referred to by the Lord as the type of His death at Calvary (John 3:14–15).

As one has said, "The *serpent* is not the type of Christ. The serpent had poisoned the people; Christ had not." The type consists in this, that the serpent hung upon the pole depicted the triumph of the Saviour over it. It pictured the fallen race suffering the penalty of death *in the person of the Representative Man*—the curse of God on those who came under the curse of the broken law being carried out in *Him*. Thus the serpent himself was defeated by the weapon of "death" which came into the world through him. This is a brief and comprehensive summary of the purpose and outcome of that wondrous death on Calvary.

Hence the work of Christ on the cross is described in the letter to the Colossians as that of a Mighty Conqueror who in battle overthrows all His foes, putting them to open shame. An old writer has a very sug-

gestive note on this passage in Colossians
—which, be it remembered again, is part
of Christ's own teaching to Paul as to the
meaning of the cross—in which he says,
"The fallen flesh has been taken possession of by the powers and principalities of
evil; it is the 'armor' in which they have
made themselves strong." So when Jesus
overcame them, He put off as He died "the
likeness of sinful flesh," and having un-
clothed Himself—"having put off from Himself" His body (margin)—"He despoiled the
principalities and the powers" and "made
a show of them openly, triumphing over
them" (Col. 2:15, mg.).

How divine the plan! "God was in Christ
reconciling the world unto Himself" (2 Cor.
5:19). The Creator in the person of His Son,
taking upon Himself the sins of the whole
world, came in the likeness of sinful flesh,
or "flesh of sin," yet without sin, so that
for the fallen creature He might open a way
back to God and become the Head of a new
race built up and formed out of His very
nature and substance. His aim was to
make us "partakers of the divine nature,
having escaped from the corruption that
is in the world" (2 Pet. 1:4).

This is the meaning of the cross in its
divine purpose, and the way of victory for
fallen man to triumph over the world, the

flesh and the devil.* This is the awful and
true inward meaning of the Fall—*the fallen
flesh was taken possession of by the powers of evil.* In Calvary alone is the antidote
or remedy. The fallen creation thus poisoned was crucified on the cross in the
person of the Saviour, so that every man
may have the option of leaving the old race
of the first Adam and begin again, "in
Christ," as a new creation.

The cross is God's weapon to deal with
the old creation (Rom. 6:6); to destroy the
fallen wisdom which set itself up against
the wisdom of God (1 Cor. 2:7–8); to bring
to nought Satan (Heb. 2:14); and eventually to destroy death itself (1 Cor. 15:54;
Rev. 20:14). Through that cross, when the
full results of the redemptive scheme reach
their complete fruition there shall come
about a "new heavens," cleansed from every trace of the revolt of the fallen angels,
and a "new earth" freed from every mark
of the curse of the Fall.

The Son of God will then see accomplished in its entirety that which He came
to earth to do, and for which it appears
the earth itself was created—that is, to be
the battleground upon which He would

---

* As the main purpose of this book is to show how the message of
the cross in the *objective* or *finished* work of Christ for us meets
the need of the world today, the *subjective* or *experiential* side is
but briefly touched upon.

enter into conflict with the rebel archangel Satan and by the sacrifice of Himself not only put away sin but, conquering the prince of this world, cleanse the heavens themselves from every trace of the discord which had broken in upon their harmony. For the tragedy of Calvary not only meant victory over the invisible forces of evil and the cleansing of the sin of man in the blood of the cross, but also the future cleansing of the heavens from the very presence of the archenemy of God and man who, through his sin, brought in sin and death from which man needs redemption and deliverance.

Far, far on beyond the Millennial age, the fruit of Christ's lonely death on the cross will have its full outworking—when "He shall deliver up the kingdom to God, even the Father, when He shall have abolished all rule and all authority and power" (1 Cor. 15:24). The revolting archangel Satan will then finally be cast into the lake of fire (Rev. 20:10), "prepared for the devil and his angels" (Matt. 25:41). At Calvary the prince of this world was judged, and all his evil works *were* brought to nought potentially, but age after age passes on before that Calvary judgment reaches its full outworking. Stage by stage, the devil is driven down from the air (Rev. 12:9), bound in the abyss

(Rev. 20:1–3), and on, far on, into the lake of fire (Rev. 20:10). For the Conqueror of Calvary "must reign till He hath put all His enemies under His feet. The last enemy that shall be abolished is death" (1 Cor. 15:26). By the cross the one who has the power of death is brought to nought and finally death itself abolished.

"And when all things have been subjected unto Him, then shall the Son also Himself be subjected to Him that did subject all things unto Him, that God may be all in all" (1 Cor. 15:28). The Father delivered all things into the hands of the Son that He might carry out the work He gave Him to do. The Father "subjected all things unto Him," but when the work has been done, and the last trace of Satan's handiwork in the heavens and in the earth is finally removed, then shall "God be all in all."

Chapter 8

THE CROSS, THE BIRTHPLACE OF A NEW CREATION

"That He might create in Himself . . . one new man . . . through the cross. . . ." (Eph. 2:15–16)

"One died for all, therefore all died . . . wherefore if any man is in Christ, he is a new creature" (or *"there is a new creation"*). (2 Cor. 5:14, 17, mg.)

SO far we have seen the cross as revealed to Paul by the Ascended Lord in relation to the Fall, to the curse of the broken law, to the darkened wisdom of man, and in its vaster scope as stretching out into realms far beyond the little planet of earth—in the final cleansing of the heavens from the very presence of the fallen archangel Satan and the removal of every trace of his handiwork in the invisible world as well as in the world of men.

Now we come to what the Lord has revealed concerning the place of the cross in His work of re-creation in connection with fallen man.

The very word "Calvary" cannot fail to move the deepest chord that can be touched in every true child of God who has been redeemed by Him who was "hung on a tree" (Acts 10:39) for our salvation. But there are many degrees of knowledge concerning all that the death of Christ meant to God, and to the world of men. To some the word "Calvary" only speaks of tragedy and suffering unparalleled for the redemption of the human race—and thankfully they bear witness to their own proving of the efficacy of the sacred blood, poured out at Calvary, to remove from between them and the holy God their burden of sin.

But there are others whose eyes are opened by the Spirit of God to see more clearly how marvelously the tragic Fall of man in Eden, brought about by the serpent—the devil—is met by the still more tragic death of the Holy One of God at Calvary becoming a *curse* for us; so that in Him as the Substitute for the sinner the ruin of the Fall is put away, and out of His death-agony at the cross is a new creation made possible.

"That He might create a new man" is declared to be the wondrous purpose of the death of Christ on the cross. The Creator finds a way, at awful cost to Himself, to become the re-Creator. The cross is therefore the exact complement of the Fall, and the Fall is the exact explanation of Calvary as it concerns the human race.

We cannot reiterate the facts too often, so that they might lay hold of us more deeply. In Eden the first Adam (see 1 Cor. 15:45, 49) fell, and came under the sentence of death for sin (see Rom. 5:12–21); and at Calvary the entire race of the first Adam had that sentence carried out in the person of the Substitute. This is the gospel of the cross summed up in its entirety. So simple is it that it can be stated in these few words, yet so vast is it in its outworking that it stretches far back to the dim and distant past, and on into the ages of eternity. Without this key of the Fall, Calvary is inexplicable tragedy; and without the fact of the Fall, the sacrifice of Calvary seems to have been unnecessary.

Bringing these stupendous facts down to ourselves individually, they may be stated simply in the words of Paul: "In me, that is in my flesh, dwelleth no good thing"—which is the "Amen" of the sinner to God's verdict on the fallen creation nailed to the tree in the person of His Son; and then follows the glad acceptance by faith of the new life in union with and under the headship of the Second Adam, the Ascended Christ.

"One died for all, therefore *all died*" is

Paul's gospel taught him by the Risen Lord; and, "He died for all, that they which live should no longer live unto themselves, but unto Him who for their sakes died and rose again. . . . Wherefore if any man is in Christ, he is a new creature*: the old things are passed away; behold, they are become new." *In Adam* the old creation is condemned to death; *in Christ* the believer puts off the "old man, which waxeth corrupt," and puts on "the *new man*, which is after God, *created* in righteousness and holiness of truth" (Eph. 4:22–24, mg.). This clearly shows that as the sinner lays hold of the declared facts concerning the work of Christ on the cross, there is a divine work of *creation* wrought in him, which consists in the imparting of a new life which was not in existence in him before.

The language of Scripture is so clear on this matter that it is of the greatest importance to understand it, lest, at this most vital point, we make void the gospel. "That which is born of the flesh is *flesh*," said the Lord to Nicodemus, and it is never possible to culture it into spirit. The theory of evolution utterly fails here. The essential natures of flesh and spirit are so radically opposed one to the other that "flesh" must fight against spirit, and spirit against the

---

*Or *"there is a new creation,"* 2 Cor. 5:17, mg.

flesh, because they are eternally "contrary the one to the other."* "Between the spirit and the flesh there is not only no *alliance*; there is an interminable deadly feud" (Lightfoot).

There is therefore no remedy for fallen man who has become "flesh" but a new birth, and the *creation in him of a new nature* by a creative act of God, wherein he is made partaker of the divine nature; and this takes place at Calvary.

That no external rite or ordinance can change or modify the inexorable fact of the hopeless ruin of the fallen Adam is emphasized by the apostle in his letter to the Galatians, where, speaking of circumcision in connection with the cross of Christ, he says "circumcision is not, uncircumcision is not. All external distinctions have vanished. The new spiritual creation is all in all."† There is a "new man," which after its creation in the believer needs to be *"renewed unto knowledge, after the image of Him that created him . . ."* (Col. 3:10).

The cross is the birthplace of this new creation. But what about the outworking of this fact in experience?

We need to understand that the work of

---

*Gal. 5:17. This is true whether the word "spirit" means the Holy Spirit or the new nature which is spirit.

†Gal. 6:15, Lightfoot. Compare Gal. 6:12–15, mg., with Col. 2:16–23.

Christ in His death on the cross could not be partial or incomplete. In the person of the Representative Man the fallen Adam has *died.* Fallen humanity was put to death in Christ for "our old man *was* crucified with Him." A writer points out that the moment when this identification took place was *after* the Lord finished His atoning sacrificial work, since in those sufferings no human being could have a share. "Christ suffered *for* sins," and in these sufferings He was alone, but at the moment of His exit from the body "He died *unto sin,*"* and to the "likeness of sinful flesh" which He had taken upon Him; and everyone who hereafter would believe and accept the message *died to sin with Him* and passed with Him into a new life, alive unto God.

The more entirely this fact is apprehended, and the believer "puts off the old man" and all his "doings," accounting himself to be "dead indeed unto sin," the more rapidly will the "new man" come into full growth and the more effectively will the Holy Spirit be able to bring to nought, or render of no effect, the "body of sin."†

But one of the paradoxes of faith must here not be forgotten. "Ye are complete in

*Rom. 6:10. The verb "die" here signifies His departure or "exodus" from the body. *Mauro.*

†That is, the entire fallen humanity of Adam, referred to again as the "body of this death" (Rom. 7:24), "flesh of sin" (Rom. 8:3), "body of the flesh" (Col. 2:11). *Mauro.*

Him," writes the apostle. The more the believer *grasps the fact of the completed work of his death with Christ as accomplished,* the more effectually does the Holy Spirit work in him to bring that completed work into actual being; conditionally, of course, upon his consenting unflinchingly to separation from all the works of the flesh (see Gal. 5:19); and conditionally also upon his active cooperation with the Holy Spirit in refusing to let sin reign in his mortal body (Rom. 6:12).

The cross is the birthplace of a new creation for every one who turns to Christ as his Saviour, but it is also in a wider sense the birthplace of the *new man* consisting of Christ and His members. Each member who becomes a new creation in his own life is but one of many units who, tempered together, form a Body with Christ as Head (see 1 Cor. 12:12–27). All partaking of one life, made to drink of one Spirit, it is "fitly framed and knit together through every joint of the supply, according to the working in due measure of each several part, [which] maketh the increase of the body . . . in love" (Eph. 4:16, mg.).

Through the cross all the *divisions* of the fallen creation are done away. Distinctions of nationality or sect no longer divide, but are part of the outward order of things of earth which are surface and temporary. For "the new man" created by God is being renewed in the believer in a sphere in Christ "where there cannot be Greek and Jew, circumcision and uncircumcision, Barbarian, Scythian, bondman, freeman; but Christ is all and in all . . ." (Col. 3:11), and also where there "*can* be no male or female: for ye all are one man in Christ Jesus" (Gal. 3:28). It means, blessed be God, that no external and temporary distinction can enter that sphere in Christ where *Christ is all, and in all.*

Calvary, therefore, is the center of unity for all who are in Christ a new creation. The more completely we apprehend that divisions and disunions between men who profess to follow the same Lord belong to the old creation, and "put off the old man with his doings," the more quickly will the prayer of the Lord be answered for His own, "that they may be made perfect in one."

Calvary, too, is the place of reconciliation between men who, according to the flesh, may be irreconcilable through prejudice, upbringing, or religious ideals. At Calvary, "Jew and Gentile" *ceased to be Jew and Gentile* as they each became members of the New Man—Christ—and so they were reconciled "through the cross," Christ having "slain the enmity thereby" (see Eph. 2:11–18).

Where the believer has really and experientially apprehended his death in the death of Christ, and learned his place in the Body of Christ—that we are members one of another, as well as of Christ—the inward spirit-union of life in Christ is kept unbroken. With Calvary as the center and basis of unity, no other member of Christ can ever be looked upon as an "opponent" while we witness to truth which that fellow member of Christ may not yet apprehend.

When all the members of Christ can see in that death on the tree their own death, not only to sin but *to all that pertains to the religion of the "old man,"* they will find a practical and real oneness with all who are one with their Risen and Ascended Head.

Chapter 9

THE CROSS
AS A SEVERING POWER

"In whom ye were also circumcised with a circumcision not made with hands, in the putting off of the body of the flesh, in the circumcision of Christ; having been buried with Him. . . ." (Col. 2:11–12)

"Ye have put off the old man with his doings." (Col. 3:9)

"Our old self was nailed to the cross with Him, in order that our sinful nature might be deprived of its power." (Rom. 6:6, Weymouth)

THE passage in Colossians which is quoted above—again, be it re-emphasized, *the teaching of Christ* to Paul, as to the meaning of His death—speaks not directly of the cross but of the "circumcision" of Christ. In this respect it more clearly brings out the thought of a knife used in the cutting of the flesh in the rite of circumcision. The words "having been buried with Him," however, center the message around the cross, for until He had *died* He could not have been *buried*. And again, it reads "buried with Him *in baptism,*" which in its spiritual meaning typified a baptism "*into His death*" (Rom. 6:3). This again centers the message around the cross, likening its power to the knife which was used in circumcision.

"In Him you were circumcised," writes the apostle, "with a circumcision not made by hands." As if to say, "the knife power of the death of Christ has been applied to you by God, who alone can perform this operation, 'even the offcasting of the whole body of the flesh. . . .'" "The casting off, not (as in outward circumcision) of a part, but of the whole body of the flesh, the whole carnal nature" (Conybeare's note on Col. 2:11).

The necessity for the knife to be taken to the fallen flesh if men were to have any relationship with God is the significant meaning of the rite of circumcision given to Abraham. It was a type of the future work of the cross when, in the fullness of time, the Son of God, having taken upon Himself "flesh of sin," would for His redeemed ones not only bear their sins as a propitiatory sacrifice but put off from Himself the likeness of the "flesh of sin" He had taken on their behalf and lead them out into a new sphere as a new creation. Accordingly, "they that are *of Christ Jesus*," writes the apostle, "have crucified the flesh with the passions and lusts thereof" (Gal. 5:24).

Here we have the application to the sinner of the power of the cross, in a "circumcision not made with hands" actually said to *have* been carried out. "They who are *of Christ*"—made a new creation by Him, so that they are now of Him, and not of the first Adam—"*have* crucified the flesh. . . ." The apostle speaks of just as real a circumcision as the Jewish rite, but carried out by no human hands. He speaks too of the "casting off" of not a *part* of the flesh, as in circumcision, but of the whole carnal nature. Not a partial work, but a full one. Not a "gradual" mastery of the sins of the flesh, but a casting off of the first-Adam life as decisively as the cutting work of circumcision.* Neither is it said to be the work of the believer, but something done by no human hands, and done in answer to "*faith in the operation of God*" (Col. 2:12, A.V.).

And what "knife" does the Eternal Spirit use but the knife of the "word of the cross, which effectually worketh" in those "that believe"! How can the "whole body of the flesh" be cast off except by the application to the believer of the truth of God speaking of the death of the Son of God, who

---

* It may be necessary to say again here that this deep knife work of God does not admit the believer into any "state" of freedom from the workings of the old Adam-life, but needs to be perpetually maintained by faith and obedience. Again, the *type* of "circumcision" fails to do more than give one aspect of the corresponding New Testament truth.

carried the sinner to His cross in His own person? The "casting off," or "putting off," of the old creation must be, on the sinner's part, the act of the will and deliberate faith in God, as the believer is shown by the Holy Spirit that message of Calvary which declares that "our old man was crucified with Him, *that* the sinful body [of the old man] might be destroyed, that we might no longer be the slaves of sin."*

The Spirit of God wields the cross, therefore, as a knife to circumcise the believer; or, in other words, to cut off from him the old creation—the "body of the flesh"—as he casts off, by the choice of his will, not a part, *but the whole*. But the experiential circumcision by the Spirit, and the casting off of the "whole carnal nature" by the believer, can only follow his apprehension of the fact of death and burial with Christ. "Having been *buried with Him in baptism*, wherein ye were also raised with Him," writes the apostle; adding "through faith in the working of God."

The true significance of the spiritual fact lying behind the outward and visible sign of baptism must ever be kept to the fore if

---

* Rom. 6:6, Conybeare. There is no reference here to the blood of Christ as *cleansing* the old Adam-life. It has been truly observed that the "blood of Christ has to do with the remission of *sins*; whereas the death of Christ, or the cross, has to do with deliverance from *sin*." The word "cleansing," if used in connection with this passage, would be misleading.

these spiritual verities are to be actually experienced by us. Every word in the Scriptures expresses a divine fact behind it, and every type, or outward sign or figure, stands for a spiritual reality. The meaning of baptism is *death*, in whichever way the outward rite may be administered. It should express on the part of the believer his testimony to a spiritual fact accomplished. This is surely true today of the Christian rite of baptism, as of the Jewish rite of circumcision. Paul said, "Neither is circumcision anything nor uncircumcision, but a new creation" (Gal. 6:15, mg.). This clearly means that an outward rite is nothing, even though ordained by Christ (was not circumcision also ordained by God?), unless the spiritual fact lies behind it in the will and *faith* of the believer.

The rite of baptism is meant to be a witness to a spiritual fact declared by God Himself: the fact that only through death—Christ's death as atonement for sin, and the death of the sinner in a baptism into His death, whereby he casts off the old creation—can a sinner enter the kingdom of God. Hence the Lord said, "Except a man be born of water [that is, typifying *death*] and the Spirit [that is, new *life* imparted], he cannot enter into the kingdom."

Faith in the working of God that the believer *is* buried with Him, having died with Him on the cross (Col. 3:3), and therefore *is* joined to the Risen Lord in His Life, must precede the casting off of the whole body of the flesh; the definite act is then borne witness to by the Holy Spirit circumcising, or applying the separation of death—cutting off the believer in truth from the life after the flesh so that he may live according to God in the Spirit (see 1 Pet. 4:6).

What the true spiritual circumcision means in experience, and how far and how deep the "cutting off" from the first-Adam life is to be, can be seen in Paul's own spiritual history, referred to by him in his letter to the Philippians. "We are 'the circumcision,' who worship by the Spirit of God, and glory in Christ Jesus, and have no confidence in the flesh," he writes, as he then summarizes the knife work in his own life, having been "cut off" from reliance upon (1) outward rites; (2) earthly dignity of birth; (3) his own moral righteousness as sufficient acceptance before God; (4) religious zeal for God. All things that count for gain to the first-Adam life are "cut off" by his death with Christ and are counted "refuse" in the light of the righteousness of God (see Phil. 3:3–7).

Paul's testimony shows that the offcasting of the "flesh" means more than being cut off from what is accounted sin, or even selfishness or the self-centered life, but includes separation from the highest ideals of the first-Adam life—from what the world calls "good." The plain fact is that the message of the cross and all that it involves means a real death to the elements of this world (see Col. 2:20), and a new birth into a new world and a new sphere with new ideals—and *new standards*. It means what the separation involved in physical death conveys to us. It means a passing from the first-Adam sphere of life by the death of the cross *into a new life* and new world altogether, wherein we declare that the world itself is "crucified" unto us, as it was to Paul, and we also "crucified unto the world."

But how long does this take to be actually carried out is the question. The well-known answer may be given: "It is a *crisis* with a view to a process." The depth of the "crisis" depends much upon the clearness of the apprehension of the believer, and upon the extent of his willingness to step out in faith upon the truth revealed to him. It depends, too, upon the sincerity of his *direct dealing with God* for the Holy Spirit to bear witness to the truth, and *to carry it out in him effectually*. For if the truth set forth is grasped and held only by the *mind* as "teaching," apart from direct dealing with God, it is likely to remain in the mind without result in the life.

Faith—real faith *in* God, and a faith transaction *with* God—alone translates the facts of Scripture into experience. As we by faith account the "whole body of the flesh" (that is, all of ourselves) on the cross in the person of Christ, and by faith in the working of God trust the Spirit of God to cut off from us all that is of the flesh—as we implicitly obey all light given and are watchful not to use our freedom for any "occasion to the flesh"—He will bear witness to the severing and liberating power of the cross.

The outworking in detail and in practice which is to follow the "offcasting" by faith of "the whole body of the flesh" is shown in Paul's words to the Colossians: "*Put to death* your members which are upon the earth. . . ." But there is to be no "process" on the believer's side in "casting off" the *sins* of the "flesh." Sin is sin and must be put away decisively and not gradually. The completed work taken hold of by faith and the corresponding "casting off" in detail make the two halves of the whole way of deliverance set forth in the Scriptures. Because they had "died" (Col. 3:3) and their life was "hidden with Christ in God," they were "cut off" by Christ's death from the world and sin and the flesh; but now the circumcising power of that death must be *continually applied* in experience, to keep them severed from the life of the flesh *manifested in and through their members*, for all the tastes, inclinations and propensities of the fallen Adam remain unchanged. There needs to be the perpetual application of the death of the cross because of the inherent disposition of the old life to intrude its workings. "So then, brethren, we are debtors, not to the flesh, to live after the flesh: for if ye live after the flesh, ye must die; but if by the spirit ye make to die the doings of the body, ye shall *live*" (Rom. 8:12–13, mg.).

Chapter 10

THE CROSS
AND SICKNESS

"A man of sorrows and acquainted with grief"—"sickness." (Isa. 53:3, mg.)

"Surely He hath borne our griefs"—"sicknesses." (Isa. 53:4, mg.)

"He hath put Him to grief"—"made Him sick." (Isa. 53:10, mg.)

"He healed all that were sick; that it might be fulfilled which was spoken by Isaiah the prophet, saying, 'Himself took our infirmities and bare our diseases.'" (Matt. 8:16–17)

THE fifty-third chapter of Isaiah was God's foreshadowing of the Messiah who was to come, and of His substitutionary work on Calvary. The marginal readings of the Revised Version of the chapter render the word translated "grief" in the text in its true meaning of "sickness." The same Hebrew word is translated "sickness" in Deuteronomy 7:15, 28:61, and some other places. This very clearly shows that the work of Christ on the cross had to do with sickness as well as sin. In confirmation of this we find in Matthew 8:17 the

statement that the Lord Jesus in His healing of the sick was thereby fulfilling Isaiah's
prophecy that He would take on Himself
our infirmities and "bear our diseases."

But if we pass on to the epistles of Paul
to discover what the Ascended Lord taught
him concerning the cross in its relation to
sickness, we find very little said about the
healing of disease in the form in which it
was manifested in the Lord's ministry on
earth. Among the "gifts of the Spirit" enu-
merated in 1 Corinthians 12, "gifts of healing" are twice mentioned (in verses 9 and
28), showing that the healing of disease by
the direct power of God was still to be
known; but of "healing" as a *predominant
feature of Christian experience and service*,
his epistles are strangely silent.

It has been said that the silences of
Scripture are to be recognized as being as
significant as its statements. If this be so,
the silence of the "Church epistles" on the
subject of healing means that we must look
for the truth of Isaiah 53 and Matthew
8:17, in relation to Christ bearing our sicknesses, set forth in another form—since
those scriptures declare a fact which is as
much a part of the gospel of Calvary as is
deliverance from the burden of sin.

The cross as the complete answer to the
Fall is again the key, for if Isaiah 53 and

Matthew 8:17 are read in the light of the gospel of the cross, as revealed to Paul by the Lord Himself, the statement that Christ "bore our sicknesses" and "bare our diseases" means that when He carried to the cross the entire fallen Adam *He carried his diseases, both moral and physical,* so that in union with the Risen Christ the believer might share in His resurrection life in that sphere where death has ceased to have dominion over Him (Rom. 6:8–11).

For the members of Christ—brought into living union with Him as Head, sharing in the death by which He died and passed out of the "likeness of flesh of sin" which He had taken upon Him, sharing also in His risen life and partaking of the power of His resurrection—God's way of *dealing with sickness is by way of the cross*, as the believer apprehends his own death with Christ at Calvary and his union with Him in His resurrection.

Thus we see again how the cross of Calvary is God's answer to the Fall, for sickness and disease came in with the Fall as well as death; and the results of the Fall find their antidote or remedy in the cross.

But how about the practical outworking of this fact? The "offcasting of the body of the flesh" is an act of faith and the will; is there some such line of action in connection with life for the mortal body?

To understand this, we need to have some intelligent comprehension of the subjective work of the Spirit in the believer's life as He leads him on into all truth; for there is not only a "present truth" for the Church of Christ in its advance to full stature in Him, but also for the believer *who is not able to assimilate truth out of the range of his stage of growth.*

It is important to remember that the work of the Holy Spirit is not only to reveal what Christ has done on the cross in carrying sin and the sinner to the tree, but also to *subjectively apply the power of that death* to the sinner himself, so that the life of the new creation is brought into full growth for the *very life of Jesus to be manifested* in the quickening, energizing, and, when it is the will of God, the *healing* of the mortal body.

Let us trace briefly the way in which the Holy Spirit generally works, for it never can be said that any order is invariable.

The Spirit of God works in the sinner from center to circumference—that is, spirit, soul and body. The first application of the finished work of Christ on the cross is to the man when he passes from death to life through faith in the fact of Christ bearing his sins on the tree. By the inbreathing of the Spirit of life he then becomes a partaker of the divine nature, for "that which is born of the Spirit *is spirit.*"

The next stage is often the obtaining of the citadel of the will for God, so that at the center of the man the Saviour is enthroned as Master and Lord. Then begins the deep inner working of the Spirit when conviction follows conviction, and the believer becomes more and more conscious of the bondage of sin. His *sins* have been put away by the precious blood of the Lamb, but now *sin* in his very nature manifests its power. The grosser forms of sin may have been put away, but now the deeper sins of the inner life and disposition—covetousness, selfishness, greed, jealousy, envy and malice, and countless other forms of sin—are brought to light.

It is now that the cross in its severing power is revealed, and the believer lays hold of its message with faith in "the operation of God." It is now that he sees God's method of deliverance from *sin* is by way of *death* with Christ, as he counts himself "dead indeed unto sin" and "alive unto God." It is now that he "puts off the old man," and presents himself unto God as alive from the dead; now that he realizes the reality of the Fall, and the fact that by his death with Christ his connection with the old Adam race is really broken . . . and that being joined to the Second Adam, the Lord from heaven, he may walk henceforth in newness of life!

This stage reached, there is yet much more for the Holy Spirit to do. The life of nature—the natural life—described as the life of the soul,* has now to be dealt with. The bondage of sin has been broken. The man walks in conscious victory over sin, and in conscious fellowship with God. The life of God within is deepening and growing, but in the increasing light of God he becomes aware of some "life" at work in his personality which is manifestly not the life of the new creation. His personal idiosyncracies begin to trouble him. He finds that his impulses are not under control: his mental activities are variable; sometimes the mind is manifestly taught of God, and sometimes its activities, or its sluggishness, or various "thoughts," are clearly not governed by the Spirit of God.

Deeper the work of grace goes on, and deeper grows the insight into the meaning of the cross and the fathomless depths of deliverance and life obtainable there. The marvelous opening up of the depths of the cross by the Spirit of God, and the unvarying witness of God to every step of faith—

---

*See Matt. 10:39; John 12:24. This aspect of the work of grace in the believer is dealt with more fully in *Soul and Spirit*.

appropriating, in fresh and unthought-of ways, freedom from the results of the Fall through the recognition of the old creation having been crucified with Christ—brings the new, more mature believer into a new attitude toward the question of sickness. The thought continually recurs, what is God's will for the "mortal body"?

Then the Spirit of God again pours forth light on Calvary; and He makes Paul the object lesson—as He once made Stephen to Paul. Through Paul is given the deeper vision of the outworking of the cross even in the "mortal body."

The great Apostle to the Gentiles does not appear to have been "healed" as the sick were once healed by Christ. And yet the life of Jesus was manifested in his mortal flesh so that he was never subjected to its weaknesses, but, on the contrary, he lived a life that would have tested the strength of the most vigorous physical frame. His cry never seems to have been for "healing," but that he might know the power of Christ's resurrection. I am "weak with Him"—for "He was crucified through weakness," he says—but I also *"live* with Him through the power of God" (2 Cor. 13:4, mg.).

This appears to be God's way of dealing with the mortal body by way of the cross for all who are joined to the Risen Christ; and this is the answer to the Fall in its aspect of sickness and disease. Just as God's remedy in every other result of the Fall is via Calvary, so disease and weakness in the physical frame is to be met by the believer recognizing that he has died with Christ and now lives moment by moment by the life of Jesus imparted to him as he abides in union with the Risen Lord.*

But does God never "heal" those who trust Him? Yes, He does, but to be healed and set free from all *physical limitations* would be for many a deadly danger to the soul. "*Lest* I should be exalted . . . there was given to me a stake in the flesh," said Paul, and "I besought the Lord thrice that it might depart from me, and He hath said unto me, My grace is sufficient . . ." (see 2 Cor. 12:7–10, mg.).

But the "stake" never hindered Paul's service for Christ. "Weaknesses" are not "permitted" by God to keep believers from service, but are bestowed as deeper equipment—making the child of God a better vehicle for the outflow of divine power. "I am strong enough for all things in Him who

---

*The question of the use of "means" is not touched upon here, as being a matter of direct personal guidance by the Living Lord, truly given to all who walk closely with Him and seek to know His will. This apparently was Paul's attitude. See 1 Tim. 5:23; Phil. 3:15. Also Romans 14:1–23 throws light upon the believer's personal responsibility toward God in such matters.

strengthens me," cried the apostle (Phil. 4:13, Worrell). "*When* I am weak, then am I strong." "Through weakness of the flesh I proclaimed the gospel to you," and "my trial in my flesh ye despised not," he wrote to the Galatians (Gal. 4:13–14, Worrell); yet it is written in Acts 19:11–12, "*God wrought special miracles by the hands of Paul,*" for diseases were healed and evil spirits cast out. Paul himself, staked to the will of God by some trial in his flesh, was used by God—probably all the more—for the healing and deliverance of others.

In this connection a well-known writer says, "Paul, in his hazardous ministry, manifested the life of the Risen Jesus in that he accomplished in a weak and infirm body prodigies of endurance and sufferings, under which the most vigorous constitution would have broken down." Others of the Lord's servants also, "while enduring conditions which ordinarily would have killed them, have manifested the life of Jesus in their mortal or infirm flesh. The physical weakness was there all the time, and *very apparent*, but along with it was a supernatural vital energy in the power of which the service was accomplished. That supernatural energy is the *life* of the Risen Man, Jesus, communicated to a member of His body by the Spirit of

Life. . . ."

This is the deeper way of the cross, which all who can drink of the cup wherewith their Lord was baptized may know. Christ "bare our sicknesses"—therefore we may be healed. But we may be called to say, like the Apostle of the Cross, "as *dying,* and behold I live." By this path we are brought to know *victory over death,* even as over Satan and sin. "Always delivered unto *death*"—that death which is in our mortal frame, and many direct attacks of death, such as Paul speaks of as his "trouble in Asia"—but it is victory *over* death as we draw upon the "life of Jesus" to be "manifested in our mortal flesh"—for "death no more hath dominion over Him" (Rom. 6:9).

Chapter 11

THE PASSION
BEGOTTEN BY THE CROSS

"Always bearing about in the body the dying of Jesus . . . we which live are always delivered unto death for Jesus' sake . . . ." (2 Cor. 4:10–11)

"Becoming conformed unto His death." (Phil. 3:10)

"The sentence of death within ourselves. . . ." (2 Cor. 1:9, mg.)

"THE climax of the Risen Life gravitates, strange to say, back to the cross; and when we have learned the power of His resurrection, we are only being thereby fitted to become conformed to His death."* This aspect of the cross of Christ brings us back to the inner spirit of the cross which Paul caught a glimpse of in the martyr Stephen. Christ died on the cross not only as a propitiation for sin, but that He might carry there the fallen race of the first Adam and bring to birth through His travail on the cross a new race, sharing His divine nature and born in His likeness.

---

*Rev. C. A. Fox, *The Spiritual Grasp of the Epistles.*

This new nature or life, maturing in the believer in ever deepening measure as he increasingly apprehends his deliverance from the old through the cross, in due time is manifested through the man in a life inspired by the spirit of the cross, working out as spontaneously and normally as the old Adam-life once revealed itself. Stephen in his hour of fiery trial spontaneously manifested the character of Christ which was in him, so that by the spirit and nature of Christ as his life he could pray for his murderers. In like manner every child of God manifests what is in him in his supreme hour of trial. If he has followed on in the way of the cross, and "by the Spirit" made to die the doings of the old Adam-life *ever seeking to obtain re-mastery over him*, the testing hour will only bring into manifestation the life of Jesus abiding in him.

This continuous carrying out by the believer of the fact of his having died with Christ, for the manifestation of the new life inspired by the cross, is clearly shown in 2 Corinthians 4:10–12. The Greek word rendered "dying" is in Romans 4:19 translated "deadness," so the text reads "always bearing about in the body the *deadness* of Jesus." This difference in translation is important, for we were identified with Him in His *death* not in His *dying*. Strictly speaking, there is *no* process of *dying* with Christ, for His death is our *death*, not our "dying," and by it we are set free to *live* with His life, and by the power of His life to bear about in our bodies the "deadness" which cut Him off from this present evil world.

Here is the cross in its severing power continuously applied by the Holy Spirit to all would-be activities and intrusions of the old creation. "*That* the life also of Jesus may be manifested in our body." The need of nullifying, or making of no effect, the old creation in order to make place for the outworking of the new is thus emphasized once more. And further, the apostle says, "we who *live*—with the new life—are always *delivered unto death*" for that very purpose. Here is the Holy Spirit carrying out the principle of the cross in a perpetual handing over to a death experience all who are truly children of God. Again the purpose is stated, "*That* the life also—not the death only—of Jesus may be manifested in our mortal flesh." The fruitage of Calvary that follows is quickly seen: "*So then death worketh in us*, but life in you." Why? Because the "death" brings the believer to an end of all resources in himself and makes way for the life of God.

How wondrous this penetrating insight

into the inwardness of Calvary by the man who first caught the glimpse of it in the martyr Stephen! It is as though the gospel of the cross taught him by the Risen Christ had now become so wrought into his own being that he understood it, so to speak, from the inside. The objective cross had now become the subjective, and the interpretation of all his life. His spiritual vision was becoming increasingly clarified, and he could see how the cross had worked itself out in his past and would in due sequence work itself out into still fuller resurrection power if he followed on to know the Lord. He had known the power of Christ's resurrection as he cried, "I have been crucified with Christ," but he sees there is still further a power of the resurrection he must yet know, dependent upon a fuller conformity to Christ's death. It is a "power of His resurrection" which appears to be the condition for partaking in a first-fruits resurrection of the body itself, as the climatic working out of life through death— just as it was first accomplished in Christ as He hung on the cross of shame; and is again accomplished in the members of His mystical body, to bring them into one life and one vision with their Ascended Lord.

Paul's language needs careful reading. "That I may know Him," he writes, "and the power of His resurrection, and the fellowship of His sufferings, being conformed to His death; *if by any means I may attain to the out-resurrection from the dead"* (Phil. 3:10–11, Worrell). The language is clear. Here is manifestly an "out-resurrection" from "among the dead," *for which a deep conformity to the death of the Lord Jesus is required.* An out-resurrection of *those who, "conformed to His death," live martyr lives in the martyr spirit of the cross,* and daily and hourly have victory over the deaths to which they are delivered. These are they who "suffer with Him," who will be also "glorified with Him" (Rom. 8:17); who endure, and will "reign with Him" (2 Tim. 2:11–12); "overcome as He overcame," and thus will share His throne (Rev. 3:21).

It may be that this "out-resurrection" which Paul so ardently desired to share in is one and the same as that referred to in Revelation 20:4–6, which is described as the "first resurrection" of those who would be "priests of God and of Christ," and "reign with Him a thousand years." John may have been shown in its complete fulfillment what Paul but caught a glimpse of in spirit, and sprang on with keen abandonment to God to know. In any case, in Paul's day *and* our day, the conditions for reigning with Christ remain the same as those which are given of the martyr souls in Revelation 20: a "conformity to death" which may mean being "beheaded for the testimony of Jesus," or a being "delivered unto death for Jesus' sake" in countless other ways; and a separation from the world which means refusal to bow down to the world-powers of Satan, or to receive his mark in forehead or hand—for example, in thought or action.

Paul is now awaiting the "out-resurrection" which he yearned to know, when he cried, "If by *any* means I may attain . . ."; and many of God's saints today may share it with him, if they too are inspired with the passion begotten of the cross to be made more and more conformable to the death of their Lord.

Let us now turn to a glimpse we are given into the apostle's life and see an example of how the Spirit of God delivers unto death those who would know the life of Jesus in their mortal flesh. This is given in 2 Corinthians 1:8. In the fifth verse Paul speaks of the "sufferings of Christ" abounding in him, and then lifts the veil over one experience and declares that he was "weighed down exceedingly," so that he "despaired even of life." The trouble in Asia to which he refers is uncertain. It may have been his stoning at Lystra (Acts 14:19–23), but his life was so filled with storm and conflict that he might well be referring to many such incidents in his martyr life (see 2 Cor. 11:23–33). The point in the passage in 2 Corinthians 1:8 is *the way in which he viewed all these "deaths" to which he was delivered.* Pressed down beyond the strength of his "mortal body" to endure, so that even his indomitable spirit drinks the bitter cup of "despair" and for a moment faces the hopelessness of his condition, he once again finds his renewal of life through the cross.

"We ourselves had in ourselves the sentence of death," he writes, but it was "that I might rely no more upon myself, but *upon God who raises the dead to life.*" If he refers to the stoning at Lystra, when he was dragged out of the city *supposed to be dead,* we read that as the disciples stood around him he rose up, entered into the city, and on the next day went on with his preaching in another place.

This incident in Paul's life, and his inward attitude to it, is not recorded simply as history but for the express purpose of showing crucified saints how the life inspired by the cross works out in practice. We may wholly miss God's purpose if Paul is to be admired and preached about today as an example whose faith and life we

may endeavor to emulate, while we fail to
see that he is a chosen *object lesson*,
through which we may see how the principle of the cross in life—in Christ conquering death and all the consequences of the
Fall—is to be wrought out in the children
of God until finally mortality itself will be
swallowed up by life in resurrection glory,
or in being changed in the twinkling of an
eye when they who are "alive" shall be
"caught up in the clouds to meet the Lord
in the air" (1 Thess. 4:17).

A well-known writer says that in view of
the coming of the Lord, the saints living
the closing days of this present evil age are
being called of God to take regard to the
matter of their mortal bodies—a position
in advance of that to which the saints of
former generations were called, whose bodies were not to experience the marvelous
change which will come to pass at the
Lord's appearing. This appears to be true
in the dealings of God with many of His
children who look for translation, and who
are being pressed by the hand of God upon
them into a faith in Him for the present
quickening of the mortal frame, which is
surely a preparation for the moment of
their "gathering unto Him" at the Lord's
appearing. Then "death" in very truth will
be swallowed up in victory. This "corrupt-

ible" shall put on "incorruption," and this "mortal" shall put on "immortality" in a moment, in a twinkling of an eye.

Just as Paul rose up with bruised and aching body from his stoning at Lystra *by faith* in the "God who raises the dead," God means His weak ones today also to rise in faith to fulfill all the known will of God in their lives. Visibly, manifestly "dying," *by faith in the Living Christ and in their resurrection union with Him,* they, too, may say, "Behold, we live . . ." (2 Cor. 6:9).

"Killed all the day long" (Rom. 8:36–37), through the express permission given by God to men to account them as sheep for the slaughter, so that they may be brought into full fellowship with the Lamb who was slain, they are at the very same time "more than conquerers"—for they triumph over all things that the fallen creation holds dear, while they are made a "spectacle" again *unto both worlds,* visible and invisible, of angels and men, as Christ was made at Calvary. Truly this is according to "the dispensation of the mystery which from all ages hath been hid in God who created all things; to the intent that now unto the principalities and powers in the heavenly places might be made known through the church the manifold wisdom of God" (Eph. 3:9–10).

Chapter 12

THE MESSENGER
OF THE CROSS

"I determined not to know anything among you, save Jesus Christ, and Him crucified." (1 Cor. 2:2)

"Christ sent me . . . to proclaim the gospel: not with wisdom of words, lest the cross of Christ should be made void. . . ." (1 Cor. 1:17)

"For the word of the cross . . . is the power of God." (1 Cor. 1:18)

SINCE the meaning of the cross was interpreted to Paul by the Lord Himself, we do not wonder that he was able to face the whole world with it, not even excepting "those of repute" in Jerusalem, who with all their prestige as men who had lived and walked and talked with Christ Himself could add nothing to it, so complete and full had been the equipping of His chosen messenger by the Lord. The knowledge that God Himself was behind his message could even enable him to go into Corinth, that center of Greek intellectualism, and boldly declare that he had determined to know nothing in their midst but the gospel of the cross: "Jesus Christ—and Him crucified."

Paul had studied secular learning at Tarsus, and was consequently quite able to meet the Corinthian intellectuals on their own ground. His Hebrew training in the Jewish Law also equipped him to speak to the Jews; therefore, every consideration, from the viewpoint of men, would say that Paul was just the man to go among them and "win them" to the gospel message.

Yes, he was "just the man," but not from the academic standpoint, for he took the very opposite course to that which the wisdom of men would determine. He deliberately decided to put aside all the advantages his secular learning and position would give him, and boldly staking everything upon the message being the "power of God," proclaim a crucified Saviour—although "Jesus Christ" and *Him crucified* would be a message of such offense to Jew and Greek at Corinth that nothing but the power of God working with him could even gain him a hearing.

And why did Paul come to such a decision, so opposite to all that human wisdom would inspire? He tells us in 1 Corinthians 1:17 that he had had specific instructions from the Lord. "Christ sent me," he says, "to proclaim the gospel, not with wisdom of words, *lest the cross of Christ should be made void. . . .* For the word of the cross . . . is the power of God. . . ."

Paul saw the cross from heaven's standpoint, for he had been taught by the Lord Himself all that he wrote to the Corinthians regarding the purpose and extent of the work on Calvary. The message itself carried its own witness. It contained in itself the power or energy of God. It needed no additions or explanations devised by human wisdom; no compromising, or toning down to meet the intellect of men—since it was not the intellect that needed to be convicted of sin, but the conscience and will of a fallen creation.

But what a battle Paul had to proclaim his message of "all things new" through the death of Christ at Calvary. The early Church consisted mainly of Jews, and no thought of the gospel message being also for the Gentiles appeared to have entered their minds until Peter was called to visit Cornelius. The followers of Christ appear to have still attended the synagogues and carried out the Jewish rites, while "a great company of priests became obedient to the faith."

Paul was as deeply involved in thought and practice in the "Jews' religion" as any of those among the early group of disciples.

But just as Moses was called aside and shown in the Mount the "shadow" of things to come, so Paul was taken aside to be shown by Christ Himself the *substance* of those shadows. He was chosen to become the revelator of the mind of God to the Church, *after* the Calvary death had taken place, as clearly as Moses had been chosen as the revelator of the mind of God to Israel, when as yet the Calvary death of Christ was only foreshadowed by the types of the Mosaic ritual.

In thought and practice Paul emerged from all these shadows and types into the liberty of the sons of God. He saw that they must all pass away, and "all things new, through the finished work of Christ at Calvary" was his message, summed up in "Jesus Christ and Him crucified." He saw that the message of the cross in God's purpose meant first the unit of the individual made a new creation; then the "twain" of Jew and Gentile—the only two divisions of the human race—made part of the Second Adam, so that *in Christ* all distinction between Jew and Gentile would pass away. The barrier of the ordinances of the Jews broken down, none of these external rites would be obligatory upon members of the Heavenly Man, Christ Jesus—each unit being free to act according to his degree of light (see Rom. 14; Col. 2:16–17), with his vision never binding upon others. "Circumcision" did not exist, nor "uncircumcision," in the sphere of the new creation.

It was long before many of the Christians who were Jews could grasp or reconcile themselves to this "gospel." Some never did, but became bitter persecutors of the man who proclaimed such a message, showing by their very actions their *need* of the gospel they resisted.

But God was behind it, and behind His messenger. The purpose of God in the message of the Lamb slain from before the foundation of the world, and slain before the eyes of the world at Golgotha, could not be frustrated by the opposition of those who could not accept it.

We, today, are in an overlapping of dispensations, just as the Christians were at the time of Pentecost and in the days of Paul. The "old" is passing, and we are moving forward into the "new." They who most fully grasp the message of the cross will be the most prepared for the new dispensation, while those who cling to anything which God has decreed shall pass away will find themselves in the position of the Judaizers in the time of Paul. Saved? Yes, they were "brethren," but blind to the dispensational purposes of God.

We have said that Paul's gospel needs to

be revealed to men, just as it had to be revealed to him. Yes, there are believers today who have no glimpse into his full message. Some see only the forgiveness of sin through the cross, and only slowly grasp any further light upon its marvelous plan of deliverance from the old creation. Paul's gospel in its fullness is veiled to large numbers, even among those who base their only hope of salvation upon Christ as their propitiation.

Nevertheless, the cross of Christ as the basis of God's purpose to make "all things new" stands, as it stood in the days of Paul. The eternal covenant between the Father and the Son, made in times eternal, stands inviolate. "Old things" must pass away, when God's time comes to make "all things new." The "old" is shaking all around us. The "old" map of Europe has already gone; for the hour is coming when the Lamb in the midst of the throne of God will receive all that was promised to Him in the eternal covenant. The kingdoms of this world will become the kingdoms of our Lord and of His Christ.

Now is the time when Paul's gospel—which is *Christ's* gospel—should be proclaimed in all its fullness, for this gospel alone prepares a *new* man for a new dispensation.

Now is the time when all who have laid

hold of any degree of freedom through the cross should heed the message in all its fullness, so that they may cast off whatever of the old creation that may be yet clinging to them and be made ready for their place in the new that is coming.

Moreover, the *world's* awful need is the proclamation of *Calvary.* Not man's view of the "tragedy" from the onlooker's standpoint, weeping over the horror of the nails and the spear, but the divine viewpoint of it, as the substitutionary work of the Triune God, in which the Father gave His Son, and the Son offered Himself for the sacrifice, through the Eternal Spirit.

God points to Calvary, and in that cross— with His beloved Son crucified upon it, set forth as the propitiation for sin—is the message speaking out God's heart toward the world. *God points to Calvary,* and in the death there of the God-Man taking the sinner with Him to the cross is the message speaking of the tragic depth of the Fall, and of the need for the death of the sinner to sin and to the world, resulting in an emergence along with the risen, ascended Lord into a *new* world and a *new* sphere. *God points to Calvary*; and in the poured-out life of the God-Man is the message to the redeemed, showing the path for them to follow in the divine and royal way of drawing sinners back to God.

Oh that men today would believe that the preaching of the cross is the *power of God!* Not the preaching of man's ideas about the cross, endeavoring to explain what one thinks the Creator meant in that tragedy on Golgotha, but the proclamation of the death of the God-Man on the cross as the power of God to *save the sinner from sin,* and the believer from the *power* of sin, the world, the flesh and the devil.

God's messengers must face the "Jew" and the "Greek" of today with this divine message, assured that no wisdom of words, no philosophy or reasoning or rhetoric of mere human wisdom, will ever make it acceptable to fallen man, except by the demonstration and power of the Holy Spirit.

*   *   *

Satan said in the far-back past, "I will be like God," and was cast down to the pit for his proud ambition. Has the gap made by the loss of a third of the angelic host ever been replaced? We know not. But we do know that the new race of those who have been re-created in the image of the Second Adam, the Lord from heaven, are foreordained to share His throne, and to be *like Him* when they shall see Him as He is (1 John 3:2).

"And I saw a new heaven and a new

earth; for the *first heaven* and the *first earth are passed away*, and the sea is no more. . . . And I heard a great voice out of the throne saying, Behold, the tabernacle of God is with men, and He will dwell with them, and they shall be His peoples, and God Himself shall be with them, and be their God: . . . the first things are passed away. . ." (Rev. 21:1, 3–4).

Oh wondrous cross, and wondrous Saviour! The fallen life of the fallen Adam has passed away in the re-creation of a new race born in the image of the Son of God (Rom. 8:29). The wisdom of fallen man in its exaltation against the Creator has passed away. The fallen archangel who fell from heaven, who drew down part of the host of heaven and then the whole race of man in his fall, is cast into the lake of fire where he can deceive the nations no more; and finally death itself is no more for ever. "He that sitteth on the throne said, Behold, I make all things new," and now "He said unto me, They are come to pass. I am the Alpha and the Omega, the beginning and the end" (Rev. 21:5–6). Amen.

MUCH FRUIT

THE STORY OF
A GRAIN OF WHEAT

THE SOUL-WINNER'S SECRET

"If it die . . . much fruit." (John 12:24)

THERE is no field without a seed.
  Life raised through death is life indeed.
The smallest, lowliest little flower
  A secret is, of mighty power—
To die—it lives—buried to rise—
  Abundant life through sacrifice.
Would'st thou know gain? It is through loss;
  Thou can'st not save but by the cross.
A corn of wheat, except it die,
  Can never, never multiply.
The glorious fields of waving gold,
  Through death are life a hundredfold.
Thou, who for souls dost weep and pray,
  Let not hell's legions thee dismay—
This is the way of ways for thee,
  The way of certain victory.

M. Warburton Booth

MUCH FRUIT

Chapter 1

THE STORY OF A GRAIN OF WHEAT

"Except a grain of wheat fall into the earth and die, it abideth . . . alone; but if it die, it beareth much fruit." (John 12:24)

THE Lord Jesus Himself is undoubtedly the One referred to primarily in this passage, but He adds (v. 26) "If any man serve Me, let him follow Me" to call the "children of the kingdom" into fullest fellowship with Himself, so that in the laying down of life they too may bring forth much fruit to His Father's glory. Not, be it remembered, in the aspect of propitiation for sins, for *"He trod the winepress alone, and of the people there was none with Him,"* but in obedience to the law of sacrifice for fruitfulness. Union with Him who gave His life as the first Seed-grain is essential to us His followers today if we are to fulfill the purpose of our being.

To trace the early history of God's seed-grains, we must turn to the parable of the Sower, the parable of "beginnings."

"He said unto them, Know ye not this parable? and how shall ye know all the parables?" (Mark 4:13).

If we do not understand how the seed springs into life quickened by the Holy Spirit's power and becomes the *beginning* of the life of God in the soul, how can we understand the development of that life and the later stages of its growth, as they are put before us in other parables? How shall we be able to comprehend the law of sacrifice as revealed in the pouring out unto death of the first Seed-grain? For true knowledge of the mysteries of the kingdom always *corresponds to the development of the hidden life of the kingdom within us.*

THE PARABLE OF BEGINNINGS

THE SOWER, THE SEED AND THE GROUND

"Behold, the sower went forth to sow."
(Mark 4:3)

The sower may be the Husbandman Himself, or His laborers sent forth at His command. In either case, we see that all seeking for souls and all sowing of the seed of life begins on God's side, with God Himself. *"God so loved . . . that He gave . . ."* (John 3:16).

The seed sown by the sower.

"The seed is the word of God" (Luke 8:11). "The word of the kingdom" (Matthew 13:19).

The written word contains the germ of eternal life. The Living Word, the Christ of God, is *hidden* in the written word; and when planted in the heart of man, a new life is communicated, so that souls are "begotten with the word of truth" (James 1:18, A.V.). "Born again, not of corruptible seed, but . . . by the word of God, which liveth and abideth for ever" (1 Pet. 1:23, A.V.).

The ground in which the seed is sown.

"Some fell by the wayside" (Mark 4:4, A.V.). "Some fell on stony ground" (Mark 4:5, A.V.). "Some fell among thorns" (Mark 4:7, A.V.). "Other fell on good ground" (Mark 4:8, A.V.).

It is the same seed, containing the same life-germ, the same possibilities—yet meeting with four different results in four classes of hearers. Oh, how solemn is this parable of "beginnings." How much depends on the start!

THE SEED-SOWINGS

The wayside sowing.

"Those by the wayside are they that have

heard; then cometh the devil, and taketh away the word" (Luke 8:12).

That which lies on the surface is easily caught away. The devil comes to every seed-sowing of the word of life! He must be there to "immediately" (Mark 4:15) snatch the seed away, for the hearer must not be given time to think. What Satan fears is *"lest they should believe, and be saved"*!

It is the *word of God* that he is keen to snatch away! Let God's messengers remember this. The devil is not afraid of *addresses about* the word, but of the *word itself*, which contains the germ of life. Addresses may be so brilliant, or so voluminous, as to contain no real "seeds"; or else seeds so scattered that they do not reach the ground of the hearts of the hearers at all.

The seed in the stony ground.

"Those on the rock are they which, when they have heard, receive the word with joy; and these have no root, which for a while believe, and in time of temptation fall away" (Luke 8:13).

These hearers received the word with joy; their emotions were deeply stirred, but these joyful receivers had "no root." How could there be deep roots without the stony ground having been plowed and the stones gathered out? The sower must not only sow the seed but he must sow it in *plowed ground.*

The seed sown on these two kinds of ground apparently comes to nothing. The hearers have passed on—possibly to be reached again by some other sower.

The seed in thorny ground.

"Other fell among the thorns, and the thorns grew up, and choked it, and it yielded no fruit. . . . These are they that have heard the word, and the cares of the world, and the deceitfulness of riches, and the lusts of other things entering in, choke the word, and it becometh unfruitful" (Mark 4:7, 18–19).

Here the seed of life has really taken root, and sprung up. It is planted in the heart, but it has not room enough to permit its full growth. It is choked with (1) *cares,* (2) *riches,* (3) *pleasures,* or (4) *the love of "other things."*

Here we have a heart which has opened to receive the word of God but which has never been *cleansed* in its desires or wholly surrendered to God. Carnal Christians, fruitless Christians—what multitudes there are! They bring "*no fruit to perfection.*"* They never reach the point of fit-

*Luke 8:14; compare Rev. 3:2, mg.

ness to be God's seed-grains. There is fruit, in the sense that the little blade of wheat begins to show itself, but it is weak, feeble, stunted in its growth.

Can nothing be done to the thorny ground, even though the "beginning" shows a possible end of "no fruit to perfection"? Yes, thank God, there can, for other parables tell how God deals with unfruitful souls. The thorny ground may yet be cleared of its thorns and the seed of life come to full maturity.

The prophet Isaiah gives us, in Old Testament language (primarily spoken of Israel), a vivid picture of the way God must deal with the life which produces thorns:

> "The Lord of Hosts . . . shall kindle a burning like the burning of a fire. And the light of Israel shall be for a fire, and His Holy One for a flame: and it shall burn and devour his thorns and his briers in one day; and shall consume . . . from the soul, and even to the flesh" (Isa. 10:16–18, mg., A.V.).

The thorns of earth which made a thorny crown for the Christ of God, and which will make a thorny path for us in following Him, must be burned. The remedy for this is simply:

> "Receive ye the Holy Ghost" (John 20:22).
> "God, which knoweth the heart, bare them

witness, giving them the Holy Ghost . . . cleansing their hearts by faith" (Acts 15:8–9).

How many receive Jesus the Saviour, Himself the gift of eternal life, who do not know that they may also receive the gift of the Ascended Lord—the Holy Ghost, the Comforter! How few know that the Holy Spirit comes to cleanse the heart and to reveal in ever deepening reality the Christ of God! If the seed of life is to reach full growth, the Holy Spirit must be given entire control in the whole being.

"When the Comforter is come . . . He shall bear witness of Me," said the Lord Jesus (John 15:26). The Holy Spirit will bear witness to the finished work of the Redeemer, and give a true inward knowledge of the cross of Calvary, furthermore revealing the Risen and Ascended Lord. He will purify the heart from its old desires by applying the death of the Crucified One, and will make the cross a *continuous power* to separate from that earth-life which produced the thorns, so that the heavenly life may grow within us to full maturity; for "the word of the cross . . . unto us which are being saved . . . is the power of God" (1 Cor. 1:18).

Chapter 2

THE STORY
OF THE SEED-GRAIN

"That in the good ground, these are such as in an honest and good heart, having heard the word, hold it fast, and bring forth fruit with patience." (Luke 8:15)

LET us now trace the story of the seed of life planted in *good soil*. The life with the most favorable beginning will come to maturity the soonest. Let us remember this, fellow sowers in the Master's service. *Let us aim at well-born souls.* Let us seek to do more careful sowing, so as to send the young converts out into the world handicapped as little as possible at the start. Nay, even more, let us remember that our own level oft-times determines the level of those we lead to Christ. A feeble tree produces sickly fruit. Let the life be strong in us and it will be strong in those we win for Christ.

The Master describes the ground as good when it is honest! *"None is good, save . . . God,"* said the Holy Son of God! *"There is none that doeth good, no not one,*" adds the Apostle Paul. A good heart therefore seems to be an *honest* heart; honest with itself and God, honest in purpose to *know the truth* and to do it.

An honest heart will not try to cloak its sins and to make excuses for "circumstances" and about "training." It will not evade the truth of God and seek to "establish its own righteousness." It will cry out, "God be merciful to me a sinner" while others may be saying, "I thank thee that I am not as other men." It is honest with itself; it honestly desires to know the truth about itself, however humiliating that may be. It is honestly willing to put away sin and to accept salvation on God's terms.

Honest renouncing of sin *because it is sin* will make good ground for the word of life, for many grieve over the *consequences* of their sin far more than over the sin itself in its exceeding sinfulness.

An honest heart "heareth the word, and understandeth it" (Matt. 13:23), because the Spirit reveals the truth when there is an honest desire to obey it—for He will deign to teach a soul beset with honest difficulties while He refuses to satisfy mere curiosity.*

---

* "Herod . . . hoped to see some miracle done by Him. And he questioned Him in many words; but *He answered him nothing*" (Luke 23: 8–9).

Honest dealing with sin, honest renunciation of all known sin, honest confession of sin, honest desire to know the truth and to do it, honest reception of the word of God without reasoning: these conditions make good ground for the sowing of the seed. In such a heart the word of God can work effectually. In such a heart the seed takes rapid root, and the word of the cross will have full power.

Honest obedience, holding fast the word of God as revealed by the Spirit day by day, will lead the soul from faith to faith in steady growth. The Father is the Husbandman. He has sent forth His Spirit to take personal charge of the one that receives His Son, and He will faithfully do His work as the silent, unceasing Operator within.

THE GROWTH OF THE SEED OF LIFE

"Having heard the word, keep it [not hurrying it into forced growth], and bring forth fruit with patience." (Luke 8:15, A.V.)

The seed need not be watched to see if it is growing. It need not be dug up to see if it has taken root. It can be left! "So is the kingdom of God, as if a man should cast seed upon the earth; and should sleep and rise night and day, and the seed should spring up and grow, he knoweth not how" (Mark 4:26–27).

It will do its own work, and conquer and make room for itself under the watchful care of the Divine Spirit. If the human sower was *purely the channel of the Spirit* in receiving the message and in ministering the word of life, the Divine Spirit will direct the seed into the right ground and the sower can go his way. It *can* be left, for it will spring up of itself, and bring forth fruit in its season, *"first the blade, then the ear, then the full corn in the ear"* (Mark 4:28).

Patience is needed. Oh, the "patience of Jesus Christ"!

"The Husbandman waiteth for the precious fruit of the earth, and hath long patience for it" (James 5:7, A.V.). He is patient over the stages of its steady development, *"first* the blade, *then* the ear." To the little green blade just shooting out of the ground, He does not speak of "falling into the ground to die." He is silent about this even when the green stalk appears and begins to grow tall. When the green ear of wheat is forming and is *preparing* to become the "full corn in the ear"—when still in its green, pulpy condition—it is far from being fit for sowing in the ground.

Patience, child of God! Learn to wait. Learn to give God time with yourself and others. "God . . . worketh for him that waiteth for Him." "Consider the lilies . . . how they grow; they toil not"—but how *we* toil in struggling to grow! How heavy we make the burden of watching, and caring for our own soul.

Depend upon the Holy Ghost, oh honest heart—the Holy Spirit who is the breath of God—to breathe into you day by day and quicken and nourish the life He has planted in you. He will watch over His word to perform it and bring forth the life eternal from blade to ear, and after that the full corn in the ear.

But *how far does He depend on me to cooperate with Him* is the question here! Just so far as to ask your utter abandonment to Him day by day, and your implicit obedience to all the light He reveals. For it is true that—

". . . you can go no faster than a full dependence upon God can carry you.

"God is always present, and always working towards the life of the soul, and its deliverance from captivity . . . but this inward work of God, though never ceasing, or altering, is yet always and only hindered by the activity of our own nature and faculties; by bad men through their obedience to earthly passions; by good men through striving to be good in their own way, by their natural strength, and . . . seemingly holy labors and contrivances."*

The Husbandman is satisfied with the blade of wheat at its proper stage. He does not expect it to immediately be "golden grain." Patience, patience, little green blade. "He that believeth shall not make haste."

Time goes on. The little green blade has left its growth to God and has almost forgotten about its growing, for it has just been trusting through the dark days, and rejoicing in the sunny ones when they came—accepting each from the Father's hand.

It has given up "toiling," and taken to trusting, when suddenly it awakens to find that it is a *full corn in the ear*! It thought it would never produce some real grains, the growth seemed so slow! Then when the grains came they seemed at first so immature and so unfit for any use. The ears seemed all husk with no grain at all! Would it never be "golden grain," it said to itself. Meanwhile the days went on. The Sun of Righteousness shone into the heart and there came the rain of the Spirit from the Father, until at last the fruit was ripe. In the sunshine there sways in the breeze on the top of the stalk the full corn in the ear.

---

*William Law, *The Power of the Spirit,* p. 169.

THE RIPE GRAIN OF WHEAT

"Fruit, thirtyfold, and sixtyfold, and a hundredfold . . . when the fruit is ripe, straightway He putteth forth the sickle."
(Mark 4:20, 29)

Let us leave the group of grains—the "full corn in the ear" to which the seed sown by the sower has matured—and follow the story of one little grain of wheat out of the hundredfold.

The little grain of wheat finds itself one of many, all bound together in cozy nests on the top of the stalk. Such a happy group, living in the sunshine, rejoicing in the refreshing showers and the lovely summer air!

"Is this the end of it all?" we ask. Is this the goal; is this the full purpose of its being? If the grain of wheat could talk we might see it looking down on the little blades of wheat just peeping out of the ground and hear it say, *"Come up here."* Or it might forget them altogether, and become absorbed in its own beautiful life "far above all," for it left all of earth when it grew up to its present position and nothing concerns it where it is.

On the top of that stalk there is peace from the strife of tongues, separation from the things of earth, and happy fellowship with its own group of grains. There is only room for just the hundredfold in the ear of wheat, and the little grain is apt to be limited to its own point of vision and to think that no other "full corn in the ear" is quite like its own!

What a picture of many of God's children who have followed on to know the Lord and have grown up with others in happy circles and favored surroundings. How bright the days, how happy the fellowship; how delightful the meetings, the Bible readings, the service of God! How easy to look out from cozy nests and to pity less favored souls. How easy to become spiritually self-absorbed. *"Holy yet hard"* is the danger here, for it is possible to be a really sanctified soul but shut in and narrowed within our own limit; a *victorious* soul, but severe on others not on our level of experience. We may know how to "work for God" and yet lack that passion for self-sacrifice which would lead us to be poured out upon the sacrifice and service of others' faith like the Apostle Paul (see Phil. 2:17, mg.).

Is the Husbandman satisfied?

Nay, He has fuller purposes for the grain of wheat. It has not yet fulfilled the cause of its being. It has reached maturity, it is true, and hitherto the main purpose has been its growth—for it has been getting for itself, and absorbing all the necessary nourishment that it might become the "golden grain."

There are now three courses open to the ripened grain of wheat:

1. *It may be garnered alone into the heavenly garner.*

"He will gather His wheat into the garner" (Matt. 3:12).

Although sifted by Satan and tossed by sorrow and trial, the Father has promised "not the least grain shall fall" (Amos 9:9). But to be one of the *garnered ones* in the great harvest of the Son of Man is not the fullest development possible to the grain of wheat. Yet how many place their own salvation, or sanctification, as the ultimate end of all their desires.

2. *It may be used as bread-corn.*

"Bread-corn is bruised" (A.V.), "nay, He will not ever be threshing it . . . He doth not crush it" (Isaiah 28:28, mg.).

The wheat that is gathered into the garner is separated from the chaff but it is neither bruised nor broken, and both are necessary for the further use or development of the ripened grain. The Father's bread-corn must needs be bruised, but it is *never crushed* so as to be useless!

May this not mean *fellowship with the sufferings of Christ*, so as to be made "perfect through suffering," for "the disciple must be perfected as his Master" (Luke 6:40)?

3. *It may become one of the seed-grains, bringing forth much fruit.*

"Except a grain of wheat fall into the earth and die, it abideth by itself alone; but if it die, it beareth much fruit" (John 12:24).

"That which thou thyself sowest is not quickened except it die" (1 Cor. 15:36).

The bruised bread-corn and the buried grain of wheat may be but two aspects of God's working for bringing "the life of God in the soul of man" into the fullest development for His eternal glory.

The bread-corn may speak of the *Godward aspect,* as the bruising and threshing brings conformity to the image of Christ. The "bread of . . . God" in the Holy Place (Lev. 21:21) signified the character of Jesus, and His perfect acceptance by the Father as the One in whom He was well pleased. It is also written that "*we who are many are one bread, one body*" (1 Cor. 10:17). The bread is composed of many grains of wheat, ground and knit together by fire to form *one loaf.* Thus are we joined to Christ our Head; and in Him and with Him, in the Holy Place, do we become the "bread of God"—"accepted in the Beloved."

The buried corn may speak of the *man-ward aspect* of the breaking forth of the divine life from the broken grain, even as it is written *"Death worketh in us, but life in you"* (2 Cor. 4:12). This seems to point to the being poured out for others upon the sacrifice and service of their faith (Phil. 2:17)—the selflessness of self-forgetfulness that others may be blessed.

To see the way the Husbandman brings this about, let us pass on to the history of the buried seed-grain.

> On the way to the garner,
> Its death is life for another.
> Willing to die, willing to go,
> Never been taught to answer No!
> Leave the fields for others, to die;
> "Faithful to Thee," its deepest cry . . .
> Then take me and use me and crush me to dust;
> Thy hand and Thy heart I'll faithfully trust.
>
> *Evan Roberts*

Chapter 3

THE BURIED SEED-GRAIN

"Another parable put He forth unto them
. . . He that soweth the good seed is the
Son of Man; the field is the world; the good
seed are the children of the kingdom."
(Matt. 13:24, 37–38, A.V.)

HERE we have another sowing quite distinct from the sowing of the seed of the *word*. The sowing of "the children of the kingdom" in "the field of the world," by the Son of Man Himself, is expressly stated.

The sowing of the *seed-grains* produced from the sowing of the seed of the word in the good ground, and coming to the full corn in the ear, is now spoken of. The Master uses His laborers to sow the word of life, but each seed-grain He takes into His own pierced hands; He can trust it to no other, and He says, "*I will sow her unto Me in the earth*" (Hosea 2:23). "Her"—*who is she?* The one He has allured into the wilderness. The one He has drawn away from all of earth to hear Him say, "*I will betroth thee unto Me in righteousness . . . and thou shalt know the Lord*" (Hosea 2:19–20). She

137

is the one joined to the Lord—who is the *first* Seed-grain.

"It shall come to pass in that day [*"that day . . . that thou shalt call Me 'Ishi,'"* v. 16], I will answer, saith the Lord, I will answer the heavens and they shall answer the earth; and the earth shall answer the corn, and the wine, and the oil; and they shall answer *'Whom God soweth.'* And I will sow her unto Me in the land" (Hosea 2:21–23, mg.).

The Creator answers the *desire of the heavens,* and commands it to pour out its blessing on the earth. The heavens answer *the cry of the earth* by giving the early and latter rain. Whereupon the earth answers the corn and wine and oil by giving them forth in abundant measure. Heaven and earth unite in responding to the will of the Creator for the buried seed-grain "whom God soweth."

Then it shall come to pass through the yielded life of the soul in union with its Lord: *"I will say to them which were not My people, Thou art My people; and they shall say, Thou art my God"* (v.23).

How much may depend upon our discerning the mysteries of God in these last days when the Holy Spirit is doing a quick work upon the earth, preparing the "handful of corn . . . upon the top of the mountains" (Psalm 72:16, mg.) whose "fruit" shall be "as Lebanon."

Surely, the word is true today:

"Behold, the days come, saith the Lord, that the plowman shall overtake the reaper, and the treader of grapes him that soweth seed; and the mountains shall drop sweet wine, and all the hills shall melt" (Amos 9:13).

Let us turn to the seed-grain and see the picture lesson, that in these last days we may intelligently yield to the pierced hand of God and permit His fullest purposes to be fulfilled in us.

Joined to the Lord—one spirit—the grain of wheat awakens to the law of its being and yields itself to the Son of God for sowing in the earth. It cries to God to make it fruitful at any cost. The purpose of its life begins to dawn upon it. It sees that there is an element of selfishness in being absorbed in its *"own"* advancement and its *"own"* growth. It shrinks from the possible garnering alone.

The heavenly Husbandman hears the cry of the grain of wheat, prompted by the Divine Spirit, and silently begins to prepare it for the answer to its prayer. He prepares it for the sowing in the ground by gently and imperceptibly detaching and loosening it from the bands that bind it to its nest.

It may appear as if He had not heeded the cry, and the little grain wonders why He does not answer; but the air and sunshine are doing their silent work. The corn is ripening unconsciously to itself, until suddenly it finds itself loosened from its old ties; a hand takes hold of it; it is caught away and dropped down into some spot of earth—dark, lonely, strange.

What has happened?

The little grain of wheat asked for *fruit,* but not for *this* strange path. Where is the sunshine, the old companions, the old happy experience? "*Where am I?*" "*What does it mean?*" cries the lonely grain. "*Am I to be of no more use?*" "Where is my cozy nest, and all that I have been accustomed to in comfortable and congenial surroundings?" "This dark spot of earth, so repulsive, seems to be injuring my nice coat; it was so beautiful in my little nest on the top of the stalk. I was so far away from earth, *so far above all.*" So the little grain speaks within itself.

Presently it is shocked to find its *covering* going to pieces. This is worse than all. So long as it could retain its exterior beauty it would not mind the isolation, the darkness, the apparent uselessness. Ah me, is this retrogression? What can it be?

Moreover it seems like "giving way" to its

surroundings. It is *broken* by them and is not able to guard itself and remain "far above all" as before. It never thought it would be moved by earthly things again.

Meanwhile the little grain rests on the faithfulness of God. In spite of these strange dealings it knows that He is a faithful God, and will lead it safely as the blind one by a way that it knows not. It cries with the Psalmist, "I shall yet praise Him who is the health of my countenance, and my God."

Poor little grain! Trampled upon in the dark earth, buried out of sight, ignored, forgotten. This little grain of wheat that was once so admired. How the other members of the group of grains looked up to it and listened with reverence to all its counsels!

Like one of old it cries, "Unto me men gave ear, and waited, and kept silence for my counsel, . . . they waited for me as for the rain. . . . If I laughed on them, they believed it not. . . . I chose out their way, and sat as chief, . . . as one that comforteth the mourners. But *now*—" (Job 29:21–25; 30:1).

Now it feels forgotten as it passes into solitude, crying, "I looked for some to take pity, but there was none; and for comforters, but I found none." It longs for other children of God who may "tell of the sor-

row of those whom Thou hast wounded."
But these seem to lack a burden of intercession, to have no anguish of heart for
suffering with others who "suffer adversity,
as being [themselves] also in the body"
(Heb. 13:3, A.V.).

Buried grain, *say "yes"* to God. He is
answering your prayers!

Maybe you were occupied with your suc-
cessful service and with your happy experience in those old days. How little you were
able to understand the temptations and the
difficulties of the little blades of wheat.
How stern you were with those who fell,
not "looking to thyself lest thou also
[should] be tempted."

How you talked to the tiny blades of
green just peeping through the ground,
stating that they "ought" to be much older
and more matured.

How "weak" you thought them because
they were bowed to the ground as soon as
some heavy foot trod upon them.

How you discouraged them when they
were weak in the faith, and did not "receive them," nor bear lovingly with their
weaknesses. How you tried to make them
see what you saw in your fuller maturity.
You did not understand how to wait and
to encourage them, and to give them time
to grow. You wanted to hurry them on, and

failed to see that they would have increased vision only as they followed on to "know the Lord."

Buried grain, you were "verily guilty concerning your brother" in your lack of "anguish of heart and many tears" over the temptations and sorrows of others. How you guarded *yourself* and feared to stoop down to earth—to become as weak to the weak, that you might gain the more!

Now learn the mystery of the kingdom unfolded in the picture lesson of the grain of wheat, remembering that it is only a picture lesson. The life of God in you *could not break forth into fruitfulness* until *you* had been broken by God's own hand. The earthly surroundings and testings, the loneliness and humiliation, were permitted by Him so that He might *release* into life *abundant* the life that had come from God.

At each stage of growth there must be the casting off of much that was necessary before, if there is to be fuller development. At the beginning, the germ of life is hidden within the outward form of the written word; the shell may pass away (that is, from our memories) but the life—the Living Word—remains. Under favorable conditions for growth, in "an honest and good heart," cleansed from all that would choke

the seed, the life progresses, showing itself in varied outward forms that may be
described as the blade, the stalk, the ear,
the full corn in the ear.

In the fullness of time the knife must be
used, for there must come the severance
from old supports, the parting with old
experiences, the passing away of outward
things that once helped us. The blades of
green, the stalk, the ear of wheat—these
were only outward coverings for a life that
was *pressing through them to full maturity*
and sacrifice for fruitfulness.

Severed from old supports, detached
from old surroundings, again the life within
the matured grain cannot break forth into
the hundredfold without a further stripping—a breaking of an outward shell that
would prevent the fruitfulness.

In honest hearts crying out to God for
His fullest purposes to be fulfilled in them,
the Holy Spirit works even when they do
not understand His working. The danger
lies in their clinging to old experiences and
old helps and old supports, when the
Spirit-life within is pressing them on to
another stage—especially if that stage
seems *"downward"* instead of "upward,"
although our picture lesson shows us that
"downward" means fruitfulness, and is *the
sequence to the "upward" path* of the full

development of the grain of wheat.

What all this means in practical experience, the Holy Spirit alone can make us understand. It is sufficient for us to know something of the principles of His working that we may learn to yield trustfully to all His dealings—that we may not *"think it strange"* when we are *"weighed down exceedingly"* so that we despair *"even of life,"* and receive as the answer to all our questionings that it is *"death within ourselves, that we may not trust in ourselves, but in God that raiseth the dead"* (2 Cor. 1:9).

MUCH FRUIT

"Except a grain of wheat fall into the earth and die, it abideth by itself alone; but if it die, it beareth much fruit." (John 12:24)

"Death worketh in us . . . life in you." (2 Cor. 4:12)

At last the grain of wheat is willing to be hidden away from the eyes of men. Willing to be trampled upon and lie in silence in some lonely corner chosen of God. Willing to appear what others would call a "failure." Willing to live in the will of God apart from glorious experiences. Willing to dwell in solitude and isolation, away from happy fellowship with the other grains of wheat.

The little grain has learned something of the meaning of fellowship with Christ in

His death, and now comes to pass the saying: *"Whosoever shall lose his life for My sake shall find it"* (Matt. 16:25).

Silently, surely, the divine life breaks forth into fruitfulness. The grain has given itself, it has parted with its "own life"; yet it still lives—*lives now in the life of its Lord.*

A buried seed-grain, it is content to be forgotten! For who thinks of the *grain,* and of all the sorrow and suffering that it underwent while sown in the dark, when they see the harvest field? But the grain of wheat is satisfied, because the law of its being is fulfilled. It has *sunk itself and its own getting* and now lives in others, not even desiring to have it known that from it the hundredfold has sprung.

So the Christ Himself poured out His soul unto death, that He might "see His seed." See the travail of His soul, and be satisfied as He lives again in His redeemed ones. Thus in God's wondrous law—the law of nature repeated in the spiritual world—the first Grain of wheat, sown by God Himself, is reproduced in other grains, having the same characteristics and law of being—"*If it die . . . much fruit.*"

THE LIFE OUT OF DEATH

"If it die, it beareth much fruit. . . . If any man serve Me, let him follow Me; and where

I am, there shall also My servant be, [and] him will the Father honor." (John 12:24, 26)
   "For ye died, and your life is hid with Christ in God." (Col. 3:3)

We have followed the little grain in its downward path into the ground to die. It has "hated its life in this world" and now its life is hid with Christ in God.

"*Where I am, there shall also My servant be.*" While it has been consenting to the breaking and stripping in its lonely, hidden path, the divine life within it has been breaking forth in life to others, and silently springing up into stronger, fuller, purer union with the Ascended Lord. "*Where I am, there shall also My servant be*"—the servant that will follow Me to My cross and My grave shall go with Me to the Father, and his "life shall abide in heaven" (Phil. 3:20, Conybeare). "Where I am they . . . *with Me*" (John 17:24).

THE FIRST GRAIN OF WHEAT AS THE PATTERN

"Now is My soul troubled; and what shall I say? Father, save Me from this hour. But for this cause came I unto this hour. Father, glorify Thy Name." (John 12:27–28)

Even the Lord Christ was troubled as He drew near the hour of desolation and suffering foreshadowed in Psalm 22. The hid-

ing of the Father's face was more than broken heart, than nails and spear. *He could
have saved Himself,* He could have spoken
to His Father and had legions of angels to
fulfill His behests, but where then would
have been the first fruits unto God and the
Lamb?

"Now is My soul troubled: and what shall
I say? Father save Me?" Nay, the Master's
only prayer could be—"Father, glorify Thy
Name."

When Thou dost hide Thy face—
Glorify Thy Name.
When Thou art silent to My bitter cry—
Glorify Thy Name.
When others reproach and despise Me—
Glorify Thy Name.
When I am taunted that God has failed Me—
Glorify Thy Name.
When I am poured out like water; when My
heart fails me, My strength is dried up,
and I am brought to the dust of death—
"Father, glorify Thy Name."

If we follow the Lamb wherever He goes,
there will surely come to us, as to Him,
the assurance from the Father: "I have both
glorified it and will glorify it again."

*"He that overcometh, I will give to him to
sit down with Me in My throne, as I also
overcame, and sat down with My Father in
His throne. He that hath an ear, let him
hear what the Spirit saith to the churches."*
(Rev. 3:21–22)

Chapter 4

THE HIDDEN LIFE OF THE GRAIN OF WHEAT

(From the Godward side)

"For ye died, and your life is hid with Christ in God." (Col. 3:3)
"Where I am, there shall also My servant be." (John 12:26)
"Where I am, they . . . with Me." (John 17:24)

GOD is teaching many of His children today the mysteries of the kingdom—doing so through the figure of the seed-grain which, buried out of sight, yet lives with Christ in God in the power of an indissoluble life.

Just as far as Christians have "hated" their "own life" in order to share in the life of the Lord, so far do they taste the "power of the age to come" (Heb. 6:5) and have the *earnest* of their inheritance—a handful of the very same life that shall be theirs in all its fullness when "what is mortal" shall be "swallowed up of life" (2 Cor. 5:4). United to Christ, and hidden in God, they dwell at the source of every precious thing, and in intercession at the throne they exercise even now "authority over the nations" and power "over all the power of the enemy," for "out of the mouth of *babes* . . . hast Thou established strength . . . that Thou mightest still the enemy and the avenger" (Psalm 8:2). They bring forth "much fruit" by abiding in living and hidden union with the Ascended Lord. They hide in Him, while, according to His promise, He abides in them and glorifies His Father through them, producing fruit that shall remain and bear the test of the fire at the judgment seat.

In Matthew 6 the characteristics of the hidden life in the aspect of *prayer* are unfolded by Him who was the very embodiment of all He taught.

1. It is prayer with no thought of what others think (Matt. 6:5).

2. It is prayer shut in with God, whether in private or public; for God's hidden ones are in the inner chamber of His presence the moment they approach Him anywhere, and they see and hear none but God (Matt. 6:6).

3. It is prayer not so much of language as of heart. They do not need to use "vain repetitions," for if they know that He *heareth,* they know that they *have* the petitions asked of Him (Matt. 6:7).

4. It is prayer sure of response, for they speak to a Father who knows their need: "How much more shall your Father . . . give good things to them that ask Him?" (Matt. 6:8; 7:11).

5. It is prayer *definite and to the point*, for the Son of God knew His Father's heart, and taught His children how few were the words requisite to bring response: "After *this manner* pray ye" (Matt. 6:9).

6. It is the prayer of a child to a Father, and in union with the other children: "*Our* Father . . . in heaven" (Matt. 6:9).

7. It is prayer that puts God's glory and God's kingdom first, and before all personal interest: "Hallowed be *Thy* Name, *Thy kingdom* come" (Matt. 6:9–10).

8. It is prayer with a surrendered will for the will of God to be done in them as implicitly, and as rapidly, as it is done in heaven (Matt. 6:10).

9. It is prayer not for luxuries but for necessities: "Our bread for the coming day" (mg.), which means a life of simplicity and contentment with "such things as ye have" (Matt. 6:11; Heb. 13:5).

10. It is prayer in the spirit of forgiving love: "We also have forgiven our debtors"— therefore we can ask Him to forgive us our debts (Matt. 6:12).

11. It is prayer in conscious dependence

upon God's keeping and in knowledge of
the terrible forces of evil and the Evil One,
arrayed against the children of the Heavenly Father in the realm of "the world rul-
ers of this darkness" (Matt. 6:13).

In short, the hidden life is just the life of
a little child—a little child living in its
Father's presence, desiring its Father's will,
depending upon its Father for protection
from all its foes, and showing its Father's
spirit to all around.

Moreover, the soul abiding with Christ
in God, is given:

*"Hidden manna" for the sustenance of the
inner life.*

"To him that overcometh . . . will I give
of the hidden manna" (Rev. 2:17).
"He that eateth Me, he also shall live
because of Me" (John 6:57).

*"Hidden wisdom" that is withheld from the
wise.*

"The wisdom of God . . . the hidden wisdom . . . revealed . . .by His Spirit" (1 Cor.
2:7–10, A.V.).
"Hid . . . from the wise and prudent, revealed . . . unto babes" (Matt. 11:25, A.V.).

"Hidden riches" only gained in times of testing.

"I will give thee the treasures of darkness, and hidden riches of secret places" (Isaiah 45:3).

"I know thy tribulation . . . but thou art rich" (Rev. 2:9).

Fed with the hidden manna provided at the Father's table alone; taught the hidden wisdom that the princes of this world do not know; given the hidden riches that can only be gained in times of trial and darkness—surely it is true that to them that love God, "God worketh all things with them for good" (Rom. 8:28, mg.), even to them that He has foreordained to be made like to the image of His Son, the First among many brethren.

Only through the testings can we enter into deep and full life in God. We can truly know our God and His abundant grace only as He brings us through circumstances that are "a good deal beyond the possible point," as someone once said. Each "impossible" point simply casts us upon the God in whom we hide. "Deep"—"dwell deep," said Jeremiah the prophet. How can we unless we have no resource but God, no refuge but in Him?

the hidden souls are then:

> "*Hidden*" from the strife of tongues (Ps. 31:20).
> "*Hidden*" in time of trouble (Ps. 27:5).
> "*Hidden*" from the storm (Isa. 4:6).
> "*Hidden*" in the secret presence of God (Ps. 31:20).
> "*Hidden*" under His wings (Ps. 17:8).
> "*Hidden*," yes, *hidden* "behind the Lord" (Ps. 91:1, Syriac).

These passages tell of a life environed by God Himself, for "in Him we live, and move, and have our being."

Finally, as regards the outward service of these hidden ones: They no longer "run" without being "sent," for their *service* as well as their life is changed. Their place is now *in the hand of God.* "In the shadow of His hand hath He hid me; and He hath made me a polished shaft, in His quiver hath He kept me close" (Isaiah 49:2).

The souls who are hid with Christ in God are thus under His full control. He keeps them close until the right moment arrives for sending them forth as "polished shafts," silent and sure. When God wields the weapon He strikes the mark, for He knows the spot to aim at in the city of Man-soul.

When not in active use they are kept hidden in His quiver, always ready at His hand. Polished shafts—ah, they need much polishing to get the roughness off them, but the Master Workman knows how to but the Master Workman knows how to prepare His instruments for His use.

The "polished shafts" are kept for hidden work, awaiting in the sanctuary, entering into the counsels of God, ready to fulfill His will.

"Verily Thou are a God that hidest Thyself." (Isaiah 45:15)

"There was the hiding of His power" (Hab. 3:4) tells us that God's deepest work is *hidden* work. He is preparing a *hidden kingdom,* while permitting the kingdoms of this world to stand until all is ready. "In the days of those kings shall the God of heaven *set up a kingdom* which shall never be destroyed, . . . but it shall break in pieces and consume all these kingdoms" (Dan. 2:44).

He is also building a *hidden temple,* for a habitation of God through the Spirit; and preparing a *hidden Bride* to share the throne of His Son. Yes, in this dispensation He is still a God that *hideth Himself,* and there is the *hiding of His power* as He silently works out His purposes, until the day when:

"Christ, who is our life, shall be manifested, then shall [we] also with Him be manifested in glory" (Col. 3:4).

"How unsearchable are His judgments, and His ways past tracing out" (Rom. 11:33).

"Thou didst hide these things from the wise and understanding, and didst reveal them unto babes" (Matt. 11:25).

"Even so, Father: for so it seemed good in Thy sight" (Matt. 11:26, A.V.).

"IF IT DIE . . ."

"IF it die," oh, hear the message
   Falling from thy Lord.
"If it die," much fruit it beareth,
   'Tis thy Saviour's word.

Would'st thou see life work in others
   Thou thyself must die.
Fall into the ground, be buried,
   Low in darkness lie.

But He leaves thee not in darkness,
   Light shall greet thine eyes,
And in glad new life and glory
   He shall bid thee rise.

Dost thou crave to tread the pathway
   And His life to share?
As thou passeth through death's gateway
   He will meet thee there.

Thou shalt learn the blessed secret.
   He shall live that dies,
From a life poured out in secret
   Shall a harvest rise.

Freda Hanbury-Allen

FROM DEATH TO LIFE

"*LOOK at a corn of wheat not yet fallen to the ground.* . . . It is itself, and has itself, and will remain itself: 'it abideth *alone*'; it is 'bare grain.' All it asks for is to be taken care of, lest it be injured and broken. It neither receives nor gives.

"'*Fall into the ground and die*'—how many Christians are passing through experiences which are filling these words with meaning! Upon the self that encased the heavenly life, hostile forces are busily engaged. These forces are of grace. They come from the cross and are ministered by the Spirit whose prerogative it is to kill and to make alive; but they often reach us in 'the ground' of poverty, trial, ill-health, frustrated schemes, stern providences and the like. It may seem, at times, as though the spirit were being stripped even to the point of not being 'clothed upon': i.e., self may be so broken that life appears to have no interest or attraction left. . . .

"But then it is that He who makes alive begins to clothe us. . . . In the midst of the trying experiences of death, we are conscious that a strange new life is slowly becoming ours. What that new life is, it would be very difficult to describe to those who know it not. The Apostle's words shall suffice: 'To me to live is Christ.' . . . In a sense never dreamt of before, probably, 'all things are ours'; and, in blessedness beyond telling, we 'bring forth fruit *unto God*'—not unto self."

Rev. C.G. Moore
Things Which Cannot Be Shaken

"We are pressed on every side, yet not straitened; perplexed, yet not unto despair; . . . always bearing about in the body the putting to death of Jesus. . . . For we which live are always delivered unto death for Jesus' sake, that the life also of Jesus may be manifested in our mortal flesh. So then death worketh in us, but life in you" (2 Cor. 4:8, 10–12).

This book was produced by the Christian Literature Crusade. We hope it has been helpful to you in living the Christian life. CLC is a literature mission with ministry in over 50 countries worldwide. If you would like to know more about us, or are interested in opportunities to serve with a faith mission, we invite you to write to:

Christian Literature Crusade
P.O. Box 1449
Fort Washington, PA 19034